organic
appliqué

Creative Hand-Stitching Ideas and Techniques

Kathy Doughty of Material Obsession

stash BOOKS
an imprint of C&T Publishing

Text copyright © 2019 by Kathy Doughty

Photography copyright © 2019 by John Doughty

Photography and artwork copyright © 2019 by C&T Publishing, Inc.

Publisher: Amy Marson

Creative Director: Gailen Runge

Acquisitions Editor: Roxane Cerda

Managing Editor: Liz Aneloski

Editor: Karla Menaugh

Technical Editors: Alison M. Schmidt and Debbie Rodgers

Cover/Book Designer: April Mostek

Production Coordinator: Zinnia Heinzmann

Production Editor: Jennifer Warren

Illustrator: Aliza Shalit

Photo Assistant: Rachel Holmes

Cover photography by John Doughty of Spy Photography

Photography by John Doughty of Spy Photography unless otherwise noted

Published by Stash Books, an imprint of C&T Publishing, Inc., P.O. Box 1456, Lafayette, CA 94549

Library of Congress Cataloging-in-Publication Data

Names: Doughty, Kathy, author.

Title: Organic appliqué : creative hand-stitching ideas and techniques / Kathy Doughty.

Description: Lafayette, CA : Stash Books, an imprint of C&T Publishing, Inc., [2019] | Includes bibliographical references.

Identifiers: LCCN 2018037259 | ISBN 9781617458231 (softcover : alk. paper)

Subjects: LCSH: Appliqué--Patterns. | Embroidery--Patterns. | Quilting--Patterns. | Fancy work.

Classification: LCC TT779 .D685 2019 | DDC 746.44/5041--dc23

LC record available at https://lccn.loc.gov/2018037259

Printed in China

10 9 8 7 6 5 4 3 2 1

Any aspiring quiltmaker should count themselves fortunate to have such an inspiring soul to guide and encourage them as Kathy Doughty.

—*Kaffe Fassett*

Kathy Doughty's fearless use of pattern and design are truly original, inspiring, and accessible to all levels to just have a go and play. If you're blessed to visit her shop, Material Obsession in Sydney, you'd understand more of her world and meet her amazing team, too. I learned so much as a textile artist by seeing how uniquely daring Kathy is to use all different patterns and colors that balance out in combinations that just seem to work and make me smile big time. If I were to give Kathy a name, it would be "Miss Motivator" for sure.

—*Brandon Mably, textile artist, Kaffe Fassett Studio*

contents

58

69

77

86

101

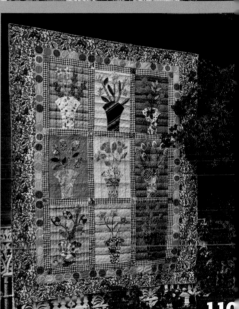

110

117

125

135

preface

Be Brave

Life is full of surprising gifts. Ultimately, it is the things we don't see coming that excite us the most emotionally, visually, or creatively. I have learned over the years to be open to these moments and to use the concept in my creative life.

On a teaching trip to the United States, John and I stopped to hike in Joshua Tree National Park. He is far more adventurous than I am and had me climbing all over the boulders before I knew what was happening. At one point, I found myself literally between a rock and a hard place, stuck on the side of a boulder and unable to move my hands or feet for fear of falling backward off the rock. I thought to myself, "This is it … I'll have to stay here until I die." Of course that didn't happen. With John's encouragement, I carefully progressed to the top (and, I admit, a few expletives were muttered). But I made it and felt a surge of joy that I had overcome my fear and accomplished something. This was an important moment, and the lesson applies to my creative process, as well!

On a day-to-day basis, *busy* is my middle name. Although I resent that I always have a million things to do, I have come to the conclusion that there is no other way for me to live. Busy is it. Every day is full to bursting. I am often asked how I "do it all." It takes a certain amount of discipline to stay focused during the busy times and productive during the slow times. Thing is, this is what I love to do, so not doing it—any part of it—is unimaginable. So here I sit with a long list of things to do but stealing time from the to-do list to compose my sixth book … the first one about appliqué. It's been a long time coming.

Rock climbing in Joshua Tree National Park made me realize overcoming my fears was rewarding.

Soul-searching is the essence of every class!

I enjoy many roles in the quilting world, including author, designer, teacher … retailer. These roles offer me the opportunity to learn at warp speed, to travel the world, and to focus on what I love to do most: design. Designing is a creative leap of faith. We find ourselves in new places all the time and must decide how to move forward. Although I love what I do, it isn't always glamorous (if it ever is!).

I am curious about how often people use the word *brave* to describe my use of fabric. I can freely admit that I, too, find myself afraid, but I continually ask myself, "Afraid of what?" To be creative we must explore the unfamiliar. Facing the fear and moving ahead toward constructive analysis of creative or technical abilities is part of the process. The trick is to be present in the moment—to see, to hear thoughts, and to feel when we are making—and in so doing we learn by doing.

I recently found myself hand quilting to a deadline in extreme heat. Despite soaring temperatures, I made myself comfortable with plenty of water and a fan. As my fingers moved the needle through the layers of my quilt, it occurred to me that the quilt had been in progress for a long time in stolen moments. My thoughts streamed through life events that had corresponded with the first sketch, then a pile of fabric, a few cut shapes, and several different backgrounds. It evolved over time, taking on many shapes. The projects that evolve over time from the first whisper of an idea to a finished project are the ones I find the most rewarding.

I rejoice in the use of symbols, patterns, colors, and techniques to make textile creations that share my perspective. As a collective, quilters share all the time. We bond by sharing patterns, ideas, conversation, and precious time as we make our treasures. After family, being a quilter defines most of my life. I am a quilter. *Organic Appliqué* is all about capturing this personal essence to be shared in quilts with pride, using thread to document our moment in time, and doing it with simple techniques. Allow yourself to make choices, to experiment, and to make mistakes. You know in your heart if you hold yourself back. Artistic expression is subjective, so if you like it, it is right. Trust your vision so you can show your own hand in your work.

Does this sound scary? If so, have a try and see what happens. Of course, I won't be offended if you make them as you see them!

introduction

Developing Your Voice

I was a late arrival to the sewing party. At first, I just wanted to make as many quilts as possible and fast! Owning a patchwork shop meant that I was exposed to so many different skills, including appliqué. I enjoyed the possibilities of appliqué but doubted that I had the ability to achieve satisfactory results. My fingers seemed to be all thumbs, and as a result my work was sloppy. It seemed as though appliqué was for those who grew up at their grandmother's knee, learning the tricks and tips that made one a perfectionist. I gave up on appliqué, believing that I just didn't have the patience or skill to accomplish this particular technique. I thought it was all about being perfect, and perfect just isn't my thing.

Time passes, and we learn as we go. Over the years, I picked up a few tips. Probably the most important was from Suzanne Cody, who said, "Appliqué is all about the preparation." Simply stated, this is the truth.

Wonky circles from *Stolen Moments* (page 69)

Preparation was something I generally avoided. Always in a hurry, preparation slowed me down until I realized that it was actually part of the creative process. A little time in preparation meant better results, and better results meant my confidence grew.

I learned to find the time.

My first organic-style projects were done in workshops with Rosalie Dace. This one, from her Branching Out workshop, really opened my eyes to original design.

Part of my voice is that I am not a perfectionist. I like a bit of a wonky line, a little bit of folksy interpretation of a shape … less detail … more feeling to engage the viewer with a style that invokes the question, "What was she thinking?" To this end, I have developed what I like to call "organic appliqué." The shapes and designs share things that I love or share stories, memories, or themes I want to explore. This isn't about making perfect shapes and putting them in exact places but rather about allowing for things to evolve naturally, with a focus on the personal rather than perfection.

Technique, or how we do it, can sometimes control our outcome as we focus only on the *how* and not the *way*. With the simple techniques outlined in this book, concentration on technique can be eased and more focus can be given to making personal choices that define the voice. Over the years I have developed a need to make every quilt express my voice, show my hand, and be unique. We all start as beginners, but the dedicated patchwork lover slowly evolves. We yearn to be more definitive. We sift through what we like and don't like to do until we develop a style of our own. Appliqué is the perfect way to create and maintain a sense of unique style.

I like to acknowledge that I am but the sum of my parts learned from the talented people that surround me at Material Obsession. I learn a lot about myself by working with other inspiring quilters, so I gather them, rejoice in their creativity, and learn from them every day.

Of course, my main influence has always come from Kaffe Fassett. He and Brandon Mably have changed the face of quilting to allow for real beauty using color and pattern. Kaffe has taught me to keep my eyes open for possibilities in the world around me—to see color and how it interacts when used in pattern.

Your Voice

I have always loved the idea that women quietly express themselves with textiles, reminding the future of their day. Cast your mind back to a day when a woman had no voice, no vote, no social power at all. The drudgery of daily chores left her alone with her thoughts about politics, family, farm life, war, and so much more. We know her now by her quilts that leave messages in signs and symbols. When considering a quilt, I often find myself wondering about the intent. What can I learn about the maker? There is evidence of social comment today in quilts regarding gun control, police violence, the environment, sexual abuse, and so much more.

ARRIVAL

Arrival is a gentle statement about a point in time when Europeans sailed to new horizons and landed under the southern stars. They found beaches inhabited only by indigenous people, undisturbed by intruders for thousands of years. Today there are those who travel by sea to new lands, hoping for a new life. They are likely to find themselves locked up or locked out. I often consider the difference between now and then with distress. How would all our lives be if those original travelers were sent back?

Early Australian quilters came on boats. If they were lucky, early convict women received a bag with fabric and needles; they were instructed to make a quilt that they could sell upon arrival to afford their first steps in life. Times have changed, but the resourcefulness of Australian quilters abounds today. Today we might just remember that most of us came by boat long ago.

Arrival (page 58)

STOLEN MOMENTS

My voice has changed since migrating to Australia. I am fascinated by how life can flourish one moment and dry to a crisp in another. As inhabitants of this land, we thrive as best we can by saving energy for the hard times and enjoying the good times when we can. We live perfectly in an imperfect land, surrounded by hardship disguised as beauty.

Environment and friends combine to create a picture of where we live … *now*. I have shared my life space with Cath Babidge at Material Obsession for over a decade. We enthusiastically fantasize about quilts we want to make or ideas we want to explore. She planted the seed of a quilt with unusual boab trees many years ago. We also share a love of quilts made by Mary Jane Hannaford, an iconic Australian quilter. Mary Jane found quilting in her 80s and made only a few quilts, but each one is a majestic display of individual fortitude. Her quilts are filled with quirky images and pieced lines of structure … treasures she left behind to inspire us all.

The boab tree, oddly twisted with a bulging trunk, lifts its branches to the sky, searching for light and moisture that will be stored inside during impossible conditions. It blooms where it is planted—just like me!

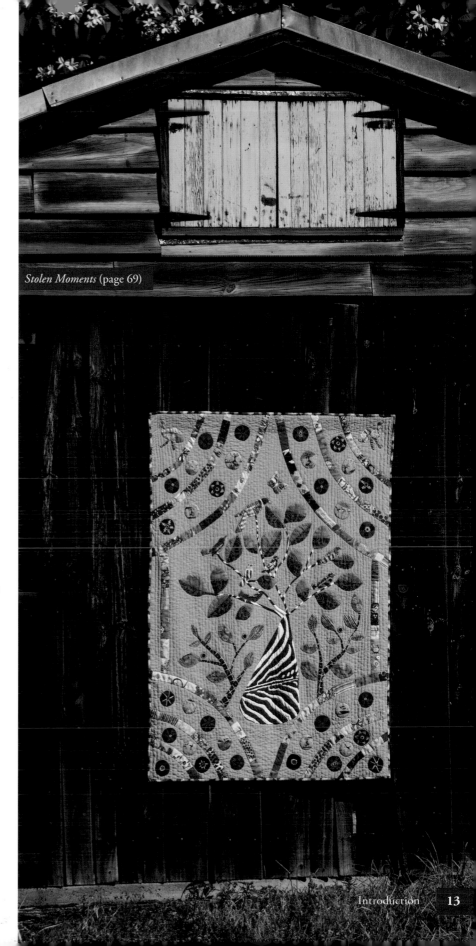

Stolen Moments (page 69)

Boro Collage (page 125)

Lifestyle Culture

One of the beautiful things about being a quilter is that we can continue to learn and add techniques to our basket of activities. From the first stitch until our last, we are acquiring experience in a variety of areas for making textile projects. In addition, we live in a shrinking world where influences from other cultures blend into our own, creating new and vibrant ideas. In the next few quilts, explore a combination of techniques that bring together different ideas using a variety of techniques and cultural influences.

BORO COLLAGE

Australia is a true melting pot of cultures. Our closest neighbors are Asian, so it is no surprise that Japanese culture plays a big role in our textiles. The *boro* technique is one born of thrift. For centuries, the Japanese have mended their clothing by sewing patches with repetitive stiches. With stitches similar to the *sashiko* or *kantha* style, it was an easy shift for me to use perle cotton #8 and apply this technique to appliqué.

One sunny afternoon in Anna Maria Horner's studio (yeah, lucky me!), I started making flowers in this method. I got to work raiding her stash for flowers that could be cut and layered. She had just designed a beautiful collection of woven fabrics that were perfect for the backgrounds, leaves, and stems. Then I made the vase and put the flowers in place. Upon arriving home, I found the Japanese fabric that I had been saving and added to the original design, growing the quilt organically. As I looked around my studio, I found other bits and pieces that could be added, and it grew and grew. Making a piece like this is very personal, and I hesitated before including it in the book. However, I enjoyed the process so much that I'd like to invite you to try it with what you may have lying about! I may even add more now!

SURROUNDING STARS

Quilting is a reflection of our lifestyle. When we are short on time (which is almost always), it is fun to have a quick session cutting and sewing on the machine. However, I work full-time and travel to teach a lot, so I don't have that many days in my studio to just make quilts. *Surrounding Stars* evolved as a travel project to keep my fingers busy during long plane rides, sitting in hotels, or while chatting with friends. English paper piecing is perfect for this type of project, as it can be sewn over conversation with little concentration. I always do the prep and then, while on the road, simply stitch whenever possible. For the last three years, the center medallion of this project has been a pick-up-and-go project.

Marg George is the pied piper of quilting in my eyes. She weaves in and out of the community of quilters, planting seeds of creativity wherever she goes. I have enjoyed Marg's presence in our classroom at Material Obsession nearly a decade. Mainly working with appliqué, hexagons, and hand piecing, her choices are well considered where fabric and layout are concerned. She was the first person I ever saw draft a hexagon! For this quilt, I have used one of Marg's paper-piecing sets. Marg's Stars have cleverly interlocked the star center into hexagons. When I make a quilt, I always have to show my hand, so I have added a surround of diamonds just to add a bit of a difference to the block.

There are several options that could be used to personalize this project. The center medallion could be a cot quilt with no borders. The borders don't have to be plaid with flowers but a personal fabric-choice statement. Or even, if you choose, the stars could travel to infinity … It is pleasurable to paper piece, and when the end is in sight, the feeling is stellar!

Surrounding Stars (page 77)

Folk Art Heart (page 86)

FOLK ART HEART

My grandmother was a folk art painter. My earliest memories of her are with either a paint brush or a martini in her hand. As an immigrant to another country, I have pined for my roots and as a result have a library of folk art books. I love the simplicity of the shapes and naive nature of the designs, which take us back to a more primitive time. When I find a topic that I like (for example, folk art), I research it online, in books, and at museums. I like to make a file of images and then see how I can twist them into a story or a project. Here we find hearts, a mermaid, a hand, and a cowboy, as well as kissing birds. They are surrounded by chain-link motifs and circles. This is a quilt that has a lot more to explore for me.

Spontaneous Starts

This is how it happens at my house: I see a fabric and immediately consider how to use it. There is a little spot in my brain that sees it, deciphers it, and decides upon a path. It might be the color, or it might be a memory awakened by the motifs, texture, or character. Whatever the reason, the result is action. I like nothing more than a Saturday with the radio on loud, my rotary cutter in my hand, and a stack of fabric that is making my fingers itch to get going! In this section are quilts that sprang impulsively onto the design wall in reaction to the fabric.

SPRING POTS

My favorite trick is to let the fabric do the work. The process is always easy, but the fabric adds interest by varying the contrast, mixing the textures, or fussy cutting. As the weather changed from winter to hints of spring, I walked into the studio and almost without a thought started designing this quilt. These flowers all have smooth lines, creating shapes that are somewhat repetitive, but the fabric makes each one unique.

Spring Pots (page 110)

ORGANIC CHURN DASH

Sometimes allowing for change in our lives brings us gifts we may not have found if we had stayed on the expected path. If we remain open to the creative flow of a project, ideas will shift and take us someplace completely unexpected and delightful!

I had a sketch for this quilt. The main idea was to use pieced blocks as a setting for appliqué. I drew up 8″ feature blocks and the corresponding measurements. When the backgrounds and Churn Dash blocks were assembled on the wall and I started the appliqué, the branches started to draw my eye as I wondered what would happen if they connected somewhere seemingly behind the scenes. I find that when something happens out of view, it is engaging for the viewer. It is hard not to look without feeling your mind fill in the lines.

Organic Churn Dash (page 117)

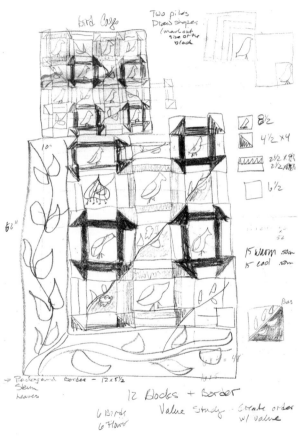

Sometimes sketches just get us get started, and then changes can happen during the process!

OVER GROWN

Summer is a time when I often find myself lost in my studio for hours ... days, even. *Over Grown* is the result of one of these sessions. Using a bit of my Celebrate collection and some special Kaffe Fassett fabrics from my stash, I got busy making a Courthouse Steps–style quilt but then got excited by the idea of adding appliqué.

One of the intriguing things about living in a subtropical climate is the rate at which things grow. A small stem sprouts quickly; cold, leafless trees turn green and burst out of their winter lines. Vines appear and take over trees, fences, or buildings in no time. The idea of growth is everywhere in summer.

The shapes are fairly organic. By layering with warm and cool colors both in the structure of the quilt and the appliqué, the result is a colorful platform about to be overgrown!

Over Grown (page 101)

Black Bird Fly (page 135)

Black Bird Fly

Some days are for fun. I am mad for plaids! When these plaids fell into my hands, I wanted to immediately get to work playing with where it took my mind as a background for appliqué. The colors are pretty and kind of frisky, so I felt free to just go with my instincts. The vertical print with stars and the trailing vine were both handy and perfect. Then the bottom yellow was perfect for grounding the project. I like the idea that the pretty pinks are pulled to earth by the grays and yellows.

The flower was from a sketch on my design wall. I started randomly cutting shapes for the petals and positioning them on the background. I wanted to see if I could get definition using larger-scale shapes. To create lines, I add in a few dark shadow fabrics to better define the shapes of the petals. I also could have used a wider variety of fabrics for the petals in a range of values.

When selecting a palette, I like to fully explore light-value to dark-value prints. The stem fabric is a reproduction-style fabric, but I liked how the strong line really stood up to the printed backgrounds. The leaves are tonal shades of green that also play against the "pretty" fabrics. The blackbirds added just the right amount of action to give the flower a place under the sun.

CHAPTER 1
seeking interest

Selecting fabric is the fun part, but it does require concentration!

Hunting for fabric is an important part of being a quilter. The practice is both emotional and technical … a right-brain, left-brain activity. The trick is not to be overwhelmed or confused by what we think we want but rather to learn to look for what will accomplish the job at hand. Rewarding choices are achieved from a balanced decision-making process with what we like and what will create the line we want.

Our stash is full of
what we love!

How often have you found a fabric and exclaimed, "I *love* this!"? Whether we are aware or not, we have emotional connections to color and design. We are all human at heart, so finding fabric that we love and wanting to keep it is pretty normal. Sadly, however, loving a fabric is good motivation but isn't always the *best* motivation. We need to be aware of what the fabric is supposed to do when placed in a project. Sometimes the first choice is the best, but auditioning other options may open new doors to better results.

It is natural to gravitate to the same kind of habitual choices when selecting fabric. In an effort to not waste time or money on the wrong choices, we opt for what we think will do the job based on experience. The end result is a stash of fabrics that all do the same thing. Safe choices including tone-on-tones, solids, and small prints are often the easiest to choose, as we can clearly see how they will perform. Most stashes are well stocked with basics, which is natural. It is a good idea to try to search for fabrics that add interest to the basics. Large-scale prints can appear to be more challenging; however, they offer a variety that sets the mood in each project, distributes the palette throughout the quilt, and draws the eye around, connecting the similar prints.

As trends change, explore the new options to see how they will perform. Fashion trends for our clothing, home, and quilts introduce brave use of color.

Creating Line

Let's start with the premise that all quilts are about creating a line. A line is created where two fabrics meet. It can be a strong line made with hard contrast or a soft line made with blending tones. Each fabric will react based on where it sits and with which partners. Understanding the relationship between the fabrics is key to understanding how a fabric will perform when combined with other fabrics. Learn to understand a

variety of prints from the experience gained in using them. Consider some of these ideas when selecting fabrics for a project:

RHYTHM AND MOVEMENT: Blocks, borders, sashing, and appliqué motifs are all created with line. Straight, curved, or diagonal lines are key elements of design in every quilt, as they direct the eye around the quilt.

SCALE/PROPORTION: Prints in different sizes will create contrast or blending in varying ways depending on how they are cut. Motif prints will perform differently to stripes, spots, or plaids. Larger prints will appear closer, and smaller prints will appear further away as in feature prints or backgrounds. The size of the piece will affect how much impact it has in the quilt. Strong impact fabrics can be used less and still be effective.

BALANCE/HARMONY: Balancing the different elements directs the eye around a quilt or a block.

Contrast

Concentrating on contrast allows us to control the lines we create in a quilt. To avoid confusion in this area, organize your fabrics for each project based on elements of contrast. Contrast can be controlled by the following:

VALUE: The amount of light and shade in any particular print. It used to be easy to pick light, medium, and dark, but with today's colorful fabrics it isn't always obvious. It is important to know how to create a value scale with your fabrics in color groups. If there are only medium-value prints, it won't be as interesting as if there are lights and darks.

TEMPERATURE: Warm colors are the reds, oranges, and yellows on one side of the color wheel. The opposite side of the wheel has the cool colors—the blues, purples, and greens. Sort these from light to dark. Creating a gradation with the fabrics provides a snapshot of the finished collection, and any gaps can be identified.

A variety of values for leaves

Exercise 1: Analyzing Your Fabric Choices

1. Select 10–15 green fabrics. Sort them from light to dark. Examine the selection and remove the darks; then replace them, taking note of how much more interesting it is to have the full-value scale. Repeat with the lights.

2. Make observations about the pile in regard to the value, temperature, and scale of the prints. The more variety in the color group, the more interest in the project.

Using a light and dark green here indicates the light source and shade while adding interest to the shapes.

Exercise 2: Looking at Contrast

Practice making two groups based on contrast elements. Where color is concerned, we learn best from doing. So the more times you practice, the easier it is to see how fabrics contrast.

1. Divide the fabrics into warm and cool fabrics and then from light to dark.

2. Select a fabric from each pile to see how strong the created line is where the warm and cool colors meet.

3. Selecting from opposite ends of each pile in pairs will show the most contrast. Selections from the middle will blend in value more but still contrast in temperature.

4. Practice making groups of fabrics and consider the points of contrast. A mixed pile will be more challenging but sometimes is a good option.

Arrange cool, warm, and mixed colors in value order to create your personal value scale. Organizing fabric choices like this is a good way to start a project.

Each color in the color wheel has many interpretations.

Color

Color is generally our first consideration when starting a project, as it is the first thing we recognize when we look at fabric. It creates the mood for the project. There are endless theories for understanding color. For many, color is a mystery, and for some a no-brainer. The tendency is to make choices that we feel comfortable with (for example, using colors we love). In fact, colors should be selected for the job they will perform in the project and not just because we like them. What does that mean? Well … it isn't about matching! It's about identifying the color and then working with all the options in regard to value, tint, shade, or saturation.

MOOD/INTENT: This is easily established with color. We will identify with the color of a fabric first, as it will set the mood or feeling of the quilt. We often make choices about color subconsciously, allowing our emotions and feelings to direct the choices. This works, but we can also use it with purpose and intent.

Collect a variety of fabric styles, colors, textures, and values for a stash that will create interest.

We are human before being quilters, so when we shop for color we tend to automatically go for the ones we love. It is often the colors that we *don't* love that are missing in our projects.

When selecting fabrics, we often try to find the exact color that is in the inspiration quilt or fabric. This is easily done when working from a designer collection. The collections are designed using a specific palette that is coordinated using the same colors throughout. The choices have been made for us, which makes it feel safe.

However, colors live in families, and exciting things happen when we mix up the expected with the unexpected. Explore a variation in value, shade, and hue in each color group. Since none of us has a perfect memory for each color, it is a good idea to shop with fabric swatches. That way you can explore different values and shades or hues of each color in an attempt to create interest. Keep in mind that there are endless versions of each color, and for interesting results it isn't about matching but rather *extending* the use of each color.

One way to achieve a good result is to group colors. For example, the three primary colors of red, yellow, and blue always work together. The same is true for the secondary colors of orange, green, and purple. That is a simple starting point. Each color then can be broken down by value and temperature. Really exploring color groups with lots of options is one way to ensure quilts are interesting.

Inspiration fabrics help us fill large areas like filler blocks or borders, and they are also useful for selecting a palette for a quilt. Look for fabrics with interesting color combinations, motifs, or graphics that reinforce what you want to say.

Inspiration Fabrics

Inspiration comes from all angles when looking at textiles. Without realizing it, we connect to the character of the print, style, or palette. There are so many different styles out there that it can be very confusing. Here, again as with color, it is helpful to consider the fabric as a tool with interesting lines and shapes as well as a sense of imagination.

Some fabrics seemingly beg to be cut into large spacing blocks, medallions, or outer borders. These feature fabrics often have a large motif or character print as well as an interesting color story. The motif on the fabric can jump-start the imagination into inspired action. The designs are dramatic and can hold space, so the bigger the print, the bigger the blocks can be. Some fabrics are particularly good for suggesting stems, flowers, leaves, and more. Consider the available choices and try to decide if they might be useful in a project for one of these reasons.

It's a lot of fun to use large prints as a stash activator, particularly if they have lots of colors. Select a large print as an "inspiration" fabric and then use it as a magnet to select a variety of other fabrics that work with it for pieced blocks.

Large prints also are a handy option for dramatic outer borders. The large print will activate colors throughout the quilt and contain them as well. It is fun to quilt around large patterns when they are used in borders or blocks, too. Prints that run along the length of the fabric are exciting when used for strip quilts or for borders. Buy the length of the quilt and cut into four equal strips along the length. Then it is easy to select a block and a stack of fabrics.

Tip Be brave! Cutting up large designs spreads the color palette effectively throughout the quilt. It is an interesting design element to have parts of the fabric motifs moving out of the block spaces. The mind becomes as engaged with what it doesn't see as with what it does see.

Choosing a Collection

A great way to compose a collection of fabrics is by using an inspiration fabric or a fabric that has interesting color combinations or a theme. Each fabric you choose should relate to the initial piece.

1. Hold the inspiration fabric in your hand and move it over related fabric options, looking for choices that are exciting.

2. Each piece you select should activate some connection between the two. Be conscious of your reaction to each combination and stay present. If it gets hard, stop and rest. I find this takes a lot of concentration.

Ultimately, it's all about if it looks good to you. Sometimes it is a definite yes and sometimes no ... and, of course, there is always maybe. I like to leave some room for iffy options and changes along the way.

Choosing Elements Within the Fabric

Another interesting use of inspiration fabric is to find areas of interest within the print that can be used to bring an idea to life.

For example, here we have a flower made with a Kaffe Fassett print. When designing flowers, we might look for pink or red, which would relate to how we think of flowers. But here, the motif from the fabric is part of the floral design. The leaves in this appliqué are a leafy print. Not exactly a literal translation of a leaf, but the print doubles the visual impact.

Sometimes the design in the fabric can be used in unusual or unexpected ways that enhance the design.

In this example, a print with teacups is used as the bell portion of the flower.

This border enhances the design by calling out to the dark lines in the pieced section and making them more visible as a result.

Scale

Using a variety of scale in different fabric prints is also a great way to add interest. We tend to gravitate to small repeat shapes, but the colorful large-scale prints have a lot to offer as well. Large prints can be engaging in that, when cut, surprising things happen. To see how a print might cut up, make a viewing template and move it over the fabric to see what appears.

Backgrounds

A variety of prints makes an interesting background in neutral colors.

Here we consider the term *negative space*, which may be a background for appliqué or the space between blocks or design elements. It used to be that we used quilter's muslin or a solid white, cream, or ivory for a background. However, as we have gotten more used to color, our needs for backgrounds have advanced to include more options. Many of our fabrics are now white based instead of cream or bone. Gray has grown in popularity for low-volume backgrounds, as it sits so nicely with color.

It is quite acceptable to use spots, stripes, or checks as backgrounds for appliqué or piecing. As long as you can see your work, any background will do—so experiment with as many options as possible. Look for regular spacing for backgrounds, as they will read more gently than irregularly spaced graphics.

Photo by Kelly Burgoyne of C&T Publishing, Inc.

Audition equal-impact prints like plaids for added interest.

Stripes and Directional Prints

Stripes are a favorite of mine. For one thing, multi-colored stripes can be used to consolidate a palette surrounding a medallion or for sashing strips between pieced or appliquéd blocks. Note if the design has a vertical or horizontal direction. Stripes cut on the bias make great stems!

Photo by Kelly Burgoyne of C&T Publishing, Inc.

Stripes and plaids add great graphic integrity and can perform in appliqué shapes nicely.

Let the Fabric Do the Work

Stripes make great stems!

Let the fabric do the work! Consider the design to determine how it might work within the structure of a quilt for the flowers, leaves, or vase.

Cutting across the stripe is easy and creates great movement throughout the quilt. Smart sashing can add interest without distracting from the main blocks.

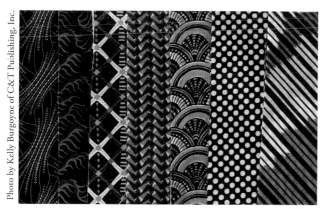

Let your imagination participate in selecting fabrics. For example, look for texture when selecting stem fabrics. Literal interpretation is not always the most interesting.

A good collection of circular motifs is always handy.

For cutting geometric or flower shapes, it is handy to have a collection of circular designs. Circles often can be used to fill in spaces or feature small motif prints.

Function over fashion works for me—it isn't always about looking good!

Storage

Confusion reigns when starting a project, but good organization allows us to get busy easily. The first step is a practical one: storing our treasure so that we can find what we need when we need it. There are as many ways to store fabric as there are quilters. It can be as simple as tossing bundles in a bucket or as thoughtful as washing, ironing, wrapping, and stacking! It's up to you, but have a think about your own preferences. This step, like all the others, is about you.

My stash is sorted into a few different categories based on how I might use them.

Consider sorting your stash by these categories:

- Color groups

- Backgrounds

- Graphics, including stripes, spots, and plaids

- Large-scale fabrics for medallions, borders, or filler blocks

When your fabric is sorted into manageable groups, you can see more easily what you have collected. This focus allows you to then consider what you haven't collected.

The simple act of sorting through the stash will reawaken your initial love of the collection and inspire you to take action with your stash!

However, the best thing about sorting the stash in this way is that the next time you go shopping you will have a better idea of what you need. In the end, you will be a more productive and resourceful shopper.

CHAPTER 2
making it happen

Dare to be different! Handwork is a meditative, rewarding process that can reflect your personal taste.

The most important thing I have learned about making quilts is that there are several techniques available for any desired result. Exploring different techniques is part of the fun of being a quilter, and it may be that at different times of life different techniques appeal. Handwork is a nice way to fill quiet moments. Slowing down and working methodically opens the mind for introspection. It's a nice way to finish off a day (or even to start one!).

Experiment to find the technique that works for you. Be honest with yourself! Some people aim for perfection, and some are happy with less fiddling around. Both perspectives are fine as long as you are happy. The important thing is that you enjoy the process!

Needle-Turn Appliqué

Appliqué sounds frightening, but it is actually very relaxing when prepared properly. You will achieve your best results when you take time for preparation. The following outlines my preferred techniques.

PREPARING APPLIQUÉ SHAPES

I prefer Wash-Away Appliqué Sheets (by C&T Publishing) for preparing my appliqué, as they are handy for both designing and stitching my shapes. You can trace designs from a pattern sheet, print them from a computer, or freehand draw onto the flat side of the paper. The beauty of the wash-away sheets is that the paper makes stitching so easy!

Wash-away appliqué paper is a commercially produced fusible paper that can be fused onto the wrong side of the fabric shape to be appliquéd. The cut paper—the exact size of the finished motif—provides a sturdy surface for turning the seam allowance to the back of the shape before stitching. After it is sewn in place, the paper can be dissolved with water. To be honest, some of these products dissolve more than others, so I leave as little material as possible inside my appliqués.

---

1. Trace or draw the shapes onto the paper. Fold the paper in half if drawing a symmetrical shape.

Tip Remember that a shape drawn on the flat side of the paper is the *reverse* of how the shape will be cut out of the fabric. Some shapes are symmetrical, so it doesn't matter. Decide if that matters, and if so, either draw the shape onto the rough side of the appliqué paper or trace it in reverse using a lightbox or window.

2. Cut the paper shape out on the drawn line. Trim away about ¼″ on the inside, leaving a narrow frame of the shape. Keep all the paper you have removed to use for extras at different sizes.

3. Fuse the paper onto the wrong side of the fabric. It is easier to needle turn when shapes are cut on the bias grain, so place the shapes on the diagonal to take advantage of the bias.

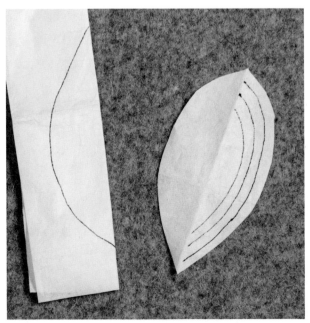

Draw the shape on the paper. I fold it in half so both sides are the same. Draw or simply cut out the inner leaf shapes and then fuse them onto the back of the fabric, leaving room for the seam allowance.

4. Cut out with the seam allowance.

5. If you are new to needle-turn appliqué, it is helpful to run a glue stick along the paper surface and then gently press the raw edge of the fabric to the paper.

Or you can finger-press the edges of the fabric to the wrong side of the shape. Doing this gives the fabric memory for the fold and makes stitching easier. Either way works.

Finger-press the edge of the fabric to the back of the paper shape. This will help with the stitching, as the fiber memory will make it easy to turn.

Tip Be mindful that the more fabric in the seam allowance, the more awkward the needle-turning process. Particularly with circles and curves, having a lot of seam allowance makes for creases and folds as well as bulky edges.

Capturing interesting elements of fabric designs to enhance what you are making can be addicting. Make your appliqué shapes special by fussy cutting or using unusual fabric patterns to make stems and leaves.

Fussy Cutting

In some projects, shapes are cut to capture entire motifs, as shown (at right). In others, look for partial sections of a print that perform differently. For example, teapots from a Kaffe Fassett fabric became the perfect flower centers in *Organic Churn Dash* (page 117).

Cut out the desired shape from a piece of white paper to make a window template (or use the leftover after cutting the shape out of the Wash-Away Appliqué Sheets). Use the window to capture details from fabrics that you might not see when your eye is focused on the full print. Once you have identified the area to be used, use a chalk pencil to trace the inside shape onto the front or back of the fabric.

Reduce the confusion for fussy cutting by making a see-through template in the shapes that you require.

NOTE

When fussy cutting, it is important to look ahead and be sure that there are enough motifs in the print to accomplish the task at hand. Hunting for fussy-cut fabrics means we need to understand the print repeat. It is generally about 24″ (60 cm). At the point of purchase, or even if you are searching your stash, count how many motifs there are before you get started so you aren't disappointed when there aren't enough. Having said that, sometimes finding suitable substitutes is a great way to add interest!

Organic Bias-Strip Stems

Bias stems are used in many of the projects in this book. I originally learned this technique from Sue Cody many years ago, and I have found it to be a simple and effective way to make stems that are unique to my projects.

1. Cut a 45° angle from a piece of fabric—the length of the stem determines the size of the piece. For smaller, shorter branches or twigs, a 10″–14″ square will suffice. For thicker or longer branches, cut a larger piece from a 20″–30″ square. If necessary, join pieces of bias to make them longer. You can cover joins with leaves or flowers if they are too prominent.

Making organic bias strips is easy using Mary Ellen's Best Press, scissors, and an iron. I like a mini iron for this!

2. Place the fabric on the ironing board wrong side up. Use enough spray starch or starch alternative to dampen the bias edge of the fabric.

Spray the bias edge with starch.

3. Turn the raw edge over, wrong sides together, and press from the outside toward the fabric to form a finished edge. This width depends on the desired size of the stem. If it is a small stem, the seam allowance can be an ⅛". Or use ¼" for wider branches or trees. It needs to be enough to give a finished edge and to not burn your fingers!

Press until the fabric is dry on both sides.

4. Fold toward the fabric again, and press from the outside to form the second finished edge. Start with a wide turn, and narrow toward the opposite end. The width of this fold is up to you and depends on how it is to be used. I generally turn it about 1" for branches and maybe 3"–4" for trees. Remember that the fold narrows toward the end of the bias edge.

The amount turned over is unique to each project. You can decide how wide or narrow the strip is depending on how it will be used.

It is also possible at this time to set in a curve. To do this, hold the narrow end of the stem and curve it. Follow the curve with the iron on the inside edge to set in the curve.

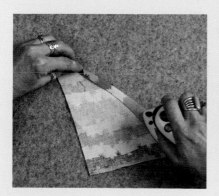

5. Use scissors to cut a scant ¼" away from the second fold. The stem is now ready for appliqué.

Cut the stem away from the fabric, leaving a ¼" seam allowance. Now it is ready to use.

PLACING APPLIQUÉ SHAPES ONTO THE BACKGROUND

Basting with Glue and Pins

1. Arrange the shapes on the background. I often use a glue stick to temporarily stick them in place. Pin in place using appliqué pins. I prefer the short white-headed ones from Clover.

2. For bias stems and vines, use liquid glue. Dot the glue lightly only where there will be more than 1 layer of fabric to avoid the dots showing through. Position the stem and finger-press it to the background.

Use light dots of liquid glue where there will be more than 1 layer of fabric in the appliqué shape to prevent the dots from showing through.

Position the stem and finger-press it down onto the background.

Thread Basting

Large appliqué shapes such as the tree in *Stolen Moments* (page 69) need to be basted in place securely so it is easier to bunch up the fabric to make the appliqué stitches.

Press the background in half along the length and width to find the center. Then position the appliqué shape on the background and stitch through the shape to hold in place. Baste about ¾″ from the outer edge to allow for turning the seam allowance to the back of the shape.

NEEDLE-TURN STITCHING

Appliqué is all about making the stitches disappear. To do this, it is essential to bring the thread up and return it to the wrong side with a vertical stitch. The needle comes up through the fold and returns in the same location, virtually disappearing. Stitches will show when the needle goes in at an angle either before or after the entry point.

Practice a few stitches. If they are diagonal, keep working at it until the needle goes straight through to the back of the work. This takes a bit of practice, but the effort produces great reward.

1. When the shape is in place, bring the appliqué thread up through the back of the fabric, just at the edge of the appliqué shape.

2. Pinch the shape and the background with one hand so that the area to be stitched is obvious. Use the needle to turn the fabric to the wrong side of the shape.

3. Bring the needle straight through the side edge of the appliqué shape and then straight down into the background fabric. For the next stitch, slide the needle along the back of the fabric and come back up through the side of the shape.

Use the needle to turn the fabric to the wrong side of the shape.

The needle should go straight through the side edge of the shape and the background. It then slides along the back of the fabric and comes back up through the side of the shape.

Inner and Outer Curves

Most of the shapes in this book are purposefully designed to avoid tricky stitching. Easy curves and shallow dips are simple to appliqué. The trick to sharp inner curves is clipping. Here are a few tips:

CURVES OR CIRCLE EDGES: Sew circles with as little seam allowance as possible. Excess seam allowance produces lumpy edges. Trim to a scant ¼″. To avoid lumps, turn the seam allowance over only one stitch at a time. The smaller the circle, the more this applies.

WITH VALLEY SHAPES, the seam allowance needs a few clips into the curve to allow the fabric to turn under smoothly. This is a bit of a freaky process. It took me a long time to actually accept that all will be well if I snip through the seam allowance to the finished edge.

1. Stitch to the curve; snip just before stitching to avoid the fraying that is caused by handling.

2. Use the needle to swipe the cut curves to the wrong side; then take small stitches through the curve. Once mastered, this is a simple and rewarding process!

Layering Shapes

Always consider the layers and make each piece before sewing to the background.

A variety of fabrics in layers adds dimension and interest. Layer the pieces and stitch together before appliquéing the final shape to the background. It is a good idea to cut away behind the shapes.

Culture-Blending Appliqué

BRODERIE PERSE

An age-old form of appliqué, Broderie Perse is a thrifty method. It is all about capturing an image from a piece of fabric to feature. You can create a design easily by using interesting scraps or limited amounts of fabric.

Broderie Perse is a great way to capture interesting motifs.

Identify the shape, draw a chalk outline, and cut it out. Cut out as little or as much of the background as you think you need.

Photo by Kelly Burgoyne of C&T Publishing, Inc.

Tip   Remember that sometimes the background color is important. A slight edge of it separates the motif from the background.

---

1. Simply cut out the shape or image you desire. It isn't necessary to completely isolate the design. Some background can be included in the cut shape.

2. Position and pin, baste, or glue in place.

3. Needle turn around the shape using the drawn line as a guide for the finished shape.

Fold under any extra fabric and continue down the side.

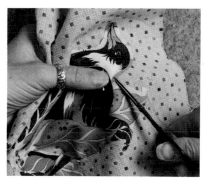

Snip inside curves.

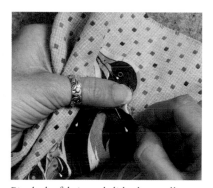

Pinch the fabric and slide the needle to turn the snipped edge to the back.

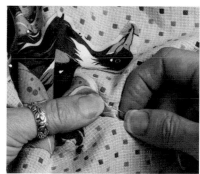

At any points, fold under the tip and take a stitch to secure the point.

A good selection of perle cotton #8 threads and some cut-out shapes of beautiful things is a great place to start with this project!

BORO APPLIQUÉ

Many cultures offer us inspiration for stitching. The kantha style of repetitive lines and the Japanese style of mending called *boro* both add texture and interest to appliqué.

1. Cut out the shape that you want to appliqué and position it on the background.

2. Use perle cotton #8 thread and a long embroidery needle to make running stitches through the background and the piece to be appliquéd. Be sure to start before the raw edge and to finish afterwards. The knot in the thread can be buried or on top!

It's that simple. I suggest that the stitches be about ¼″–½″ apart so that there is room for quilting stitches as well.

Pinch the fabric together and gather 5–6 stitches onto the needle.

Gather and stitch, pull the needle through, and gather and stitch again, being sure there is no remaining tension from the gathering.

Be sure to allow space for quilting when the time comes.

English Paper Piecing

English paper piecing is one of the oldest forms of patchwork and has a strong English influence. Fantastic commercially produced paper pieces are available, which make it easy to get started. Using precut paper pieces for shapes is a perfect way to add accurate pieced designs to a project.

Marg's Stars and Mrs. Peach blocks are paper-piecing sets that were designed by Marg George and are used with her permission. Marg's focus is on interpreting antique quilts with a personal flair.

Marg's Star blocks in *Surrounding Stars* (page 77)

Mrs. Peach blocks in *Arrival* (page 58)

I suggest using a glue stick to attach the papers to the wrong side of the fabric. If you use just a touch of the glue stick, you can easily remove the papers and reuse them later.

As in all my projects—even with the precut papers—I like to play with the design. My first question is always "How can I make it different or unique by adding a shape or taking something away?"

In *Surrounding Stars* (page 77), I surrounded each of Marg's Star blocks with striped diamonds and then set the blocks together with hexagons. The twist on the shape allows for interesting pattern play.

Basic star shape for Marg's Stars with striped diamonds and hexagons

In *Arrival* (page 58), I modified the Mrs. Peach block, leaving out the triangles that would have been placed between each spoke. The open spokes were assembled with traditional English paper-piecing methods and then appliquéd directly onto the left side of the quilt.

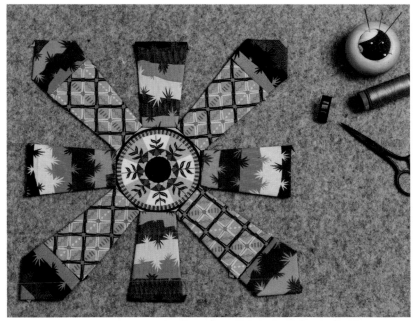

I modified the Mrs. Peach block for the border of *Arrival*.

ASSEMBLING ENGLISH PAPER-PIECED BLOCKS

1. Use the paper piece as a template to cut out the fabric with a scant ¼" seam allowance.

2. Place the paper shape on the wrong side of the fabric and run the glue stick just next to the cut edge. Finger-press the fabric edge onto the glue.

3. Arrange the prepared shapes in position. It helps to work on only 1 block at a time.

---

4. Pick up 2 pieces with adjoining sides together. Lay the shapes out flat and clip them together; then stitch across the join. Keeping the pieces flat while stitching will help to make the stitches disappear.

5. Continue adding pieces, keeping the shapes flat as you stitch. Start at the center of the block and work outward.

With adjoining sides together and the shapes out flat, stitch across the join.

Start with a star point. Add 1 partial hexagon shape and then the next.

---

6. When you have the blocks together, lay out the elements of the quilt to observe fabric and color placement. Stitch the blocks together in the same way you added individual pieces: Lay the shapes out flat, with the edges matching, and stitch over the seam join.

7. Spray with Best Press and press until dry. Do not remove the papers until they are about to be appliquéd to the background.

8. To finish a project using paper pieces, there are several options. See *Surrounding Stars* (page 77) to see how to appliqué a medallion or any centerpiece to a frame.

Some fabrics beg to be used big! Dynamic prints, directional prints, or specific palettes can be just what you need for a border to bring it home perfectly!

Photo by Kelly Burgoyne of C&T Publishing, Inc.

Adding Borders

One of the most important lessons in my early quilting life was how to add borders. Here's the thing—as we sew, no matter how hard we try to be accurate, we change the finished measurements of any quilt. In order to keep projects square, it is important to follow some simple steps:

1. Measure the length and width of the blocks/quilt through the center. This is your true measurement.

2. Cut your borders to this measurement, regardless of instructions that differ. Start by adding the side borders *or* the top and bottom borders. Find the center of the border and the center of the quilt body. Match the centers and pin; then pin the ends together. Add pins along the length, easing and/or stretching to make the border strip meet the body exactly.

3. Repeat the measurement process to determine the length of the next set of borders. Following this method will help to avoid those nasty curved borders that are impossible to quilt out!

Hand Quilting

Hand quilting is a meditative practice that is the perfect way to end any day. I generally have an on-the-go project for the quiet moments at the end of the day, and I can't wait to get at it! If you are just starting, allow yourself some time to get the rhythm. I find that it is always awkward at first for beginners, but with little to no time, the stitches assume an even length and satisfaction is found!

My preferred method of quilting is with perle cotton #8 and an organic flow of stitching. I generally use Wonderfil's Eleganza perle cotton #8, as it comes in beautiful colors both solid and variegated. The threads are a very good quality and don't weaken with use.

QUILTING STEPS

1. Start by threading a quilting needle with a length of thread that is no longer than the distance from your hand to your elbow. Make a small knot at the end of the thread.

2. Decide where you want to quilt and draw a line with a chalk pencil. You can use a ruler to make straight lines or use an organic curved line if you prefer. Straight lines are easiest, so it's best to start there and progress to curves when you have mastered the stitch.

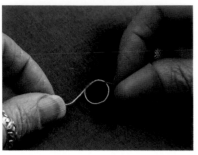

Knot the thread.

Draw a line with a chalk pencil.

3. From the top of the fabric, position the needle about 1″ from where you want the stitching to start. Push the needle into the batting, between the quilt top and the backing; then bring it up where you want the stitch. Pull the thread until the knot is at the surface. Place your finger over the knot and give it a gentle tug to pull it into the batting.

Start about 1″ away and come up where you want to start stitching. I use a rubber thumb cover to help get a grip on my needle when quilting with perle #8.

4. Position the needle so that it is perpendicular to the quilt top, and slide it through to the underside. Feel it with the index finger under the quilt, and start to angle it back to the top surface.

Going straight down through the 3 layers helps to get a nice stitch on the back of the quilt. If the needle goes through at an angle, the backstitch will be small.

Tip   Quilting does pull the background and batting in, so it is best to start somewhere in the middle of the quilt. If you are quilting straight lines in kantha style (page 42), it is possible to start at the top of the quilt and quilt down through the quilt. Return to the top after completing the length. I often use several needles at once when doing this style.

5. When the tip of the needle touches the index finger, push the needle into the lip of the thimble. Guide it back to the surface with the index finger.

Position the finger underneath, directly beneath where the needle is going through, and push up.

---

6. Use the lip of the thimble to move the needle back into the fabric to make 3–4 running stitches while using the thumb of the quilting hand to hold the needle steady.

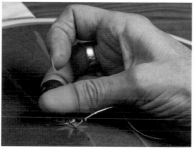

Control the length of the stitch with the lip of the thimble. Clover Open Sided Thimbles with a lip are best!

I use a rubber thumb cover to help grip the needle as I push it into the lip of the thimble and again when pulling the needle through.

The index and middle fingers underneath work to create a valley for each stitch.

---

7. Drop the thumb down below the needle and use the thimble to push the needle through. Repeat the process of adding stitches 2–3 at a time.

Tip Repeating the stitches on the needle helps you stitch in a straight line. It also helps you to see the length of the stiches. Don't worry if your stitches are big or uneven at first. Practice on a small project to avoid being overwhelmed!

Use the thimble to push stitches through.

FINISHING OFF

1. When the stitching row is finished, make a backward stitch through the batting only and bring the needle back up through the original hole.

Make a backward stitch.

2. Pull the thread gently away from the stitch to flatten.

3. Slide the needle through the stitch and make a loop.

Pull the thread gently.

Slide the needle under the stitch and then go through the loop.

4. Pull the stitch loosely to gather up the excess thread, and return the needle to the original entry point.

5. Pull the needle through about 1″ away from the hole and cut the thread to finish. Trim the remaining threads.

Tip It is critical that you do not catch any backing fabric or thread when entering the original hole the second and third time.

Return to the original hole for the third time and come up about 1″ away.

Trim the remaining threads.

Handy Tools

As with any patchwork technique, the correct tools are very helpful toward achieving a good result. Feel free to make your own choices; I am suggesting products that have worked well for improving my results.

WASH-AWAY APPLIQUÉ PAPER: When I found Wash-Away Appliqué Sheets (by C&T Publishing), I found a whole new world of appliqué. You can trace or draw on the paper or run the paper through an inkjet printer, fuse it to your background fabric, and leave it in place after you appliqué. The paper dissolves in water.

GLUE: Glue sticks are handy for paper piecing and temporary placement of appliqué shapes. Liquid glue is good for double-thickness positioning, like stems.

SPRAY STARCH / STARCH ALTERNATIVE: I recommend Mary Ellen's Best Press.

MINI IRON: This is handy for appliqué preparation and small enough to sit on the cutting table.

WOOL FELT IRONING PAD: A portable pressing surface for appliqué prep, this also works well for pressing finished appliqué from the wrong side so you don't lose the dimension of your work.

CLOVER WONDER CLIPS: These are handy for paper piecing, binding, and holding two things together when sewing.

SCISSORS: I recommend Karen Kay Buckley's Perfect Scissors.

CLOVER FLOWER-HEAD PINS: These pins are handy for sewing, as they are easy to handle.

APPLIQUÉ PINS: These are a must! They are short, so you can manage curves easily when pinning shapes in place. I prefer the white-headed ones from Clover.

NEEDLES: There are many brands of needles on the market. Select a good-quality needle from a specialty store.

THREAD: I use Aurifil 80 weight for appliqué and 50 weight for paper piecing and general sewing.

QUILTING HOOP: Use a good-quality wooden quilting hoop 14″ in diameter.

CHALK PENCILS: I highly recommend using a Bohin Chalk Pencil, the wide crayon version, for temporary lines in appliqué and quilting.

QUILTING THREADS: I use Wonderfil's Eleganza perle cotton #8—the Sue Spargo line.

CLOVER OPEN SIDED THIMBLE: This product is perfect for quilting sessions.

THIMBLETTES / RUBBER FINGERTIPS: These are readily available in office stores. Using them while quilting with perle #8 helps you get a grip on the needle; this is helpful with the thicker thread.

CHAPTER 3

design and layout

The flexibility of working on a design wall is critical to my process. The flat surface shows the lines of the work. So much of what we do is up close, and things look very different on the wall! The design wall helps me manage relationships in scale, balance, and proportion.

There is a time and a place for all intent. Making quilts from patterns and kits gives us great certainty and comfort. We know what to expect. We know where we are going, and it feels good to know we are not wasting time working out details or making mistakes.

However, I am a designer. I prefer not to follow directions or make the same thing twice! In the early days of my quilting life, I got tired of not getting the results I wanted because I made a mistake somewhere in the process. As a self-taught quilter, there was so much I didn't naturally understand. Eventually, I realized that the mistakes were treasures. Veering off the path of intent into something new often revealed something completely unique. As soon as I realized that, I opened my mind to possibilities.

Inspiration

Keep your eyes open for interesting shapes in nature that show where light and shade belong.

Look for interesting lines in nature.

A photo can offer a beautiful natural palette.

So what is the process for designing? Generally it starts from one of three places:

- Images, colors, and layouts that communicate an idea, story, or event

- A piece of fabric or a collection that inspires

- A technique or skill to explore

The projects in this book are inspired by these three main ideas using appliqué to create unique projects. My intent is that you see a starting point for your own voice, a manner in which to use fabrics, or a technique that you want to explore in these projects. Feel free to make them as you see them or to explore the techniques as presented to help you define your own voice or style.

Key to my design method is using a design wall. My studio has polyester batting tacked to the wall. By cutting and placing shapes on the wall, I can clearly see how a project is developing. When the pieces are displayed on the wall, the balance of color, value, and shape is clearly visible.

I often use my camera to photograph different stages of a project. A photograph in black and white ensures the value is working and that the intended pattern is visible. Photographs also allow us to get an idea of a project's balance, which is not as easy to see with the naked eye.

What are we focusing on?

A photo of a quilt in black and white changes the perception to focus on the lines.

Design Concepts

There is a world of advice on techniques for design. I have a few principles that I follow in my process.

- Odd numbers are visually more interesting than even (see *Boro Collage*, page 125).

- Fully explore the value scale—light to dark.

- Use the golden mean, or the principle of thirds (see *Black Bird Fly*, page 135).

- Diagonal lines are more interesting than parallel.

- The darkest blocks or fabrics sit comfortably in the bottom right side.

- Consider a variety of neutral options: browns, grays, and regular prints (see *Organic Churn Dash*, page 117).

- Balance intense, attention-seeking fabrics with earthy colors (see *Stolen Moments*, page 69).

- Consider contrast elements.

- Perspective and scale in natural order add to the integrity of a project. Blown-out perspective or scale are interesting to explore for more artistic results (see *Over Grown*, page 101).

- Listen to your own thoughts (see *Arrival*, page 58).

- Most importantly, if you like it, it's okay!

How I See It … If you consider elements of design, you can create whatever you want, even using print fabrics!

Practical Design Tools

GRAPH PAPER: Sketch out your design using graph paper to figure out the math. The process of drawing a design on graph paper helps you to keep scale in mind at all times.

CAMERA: A photo of a work in progress can alert you to areas that are not obvious to the eye. Take a photo to review perspective, balance, and composition.

DESIGN WALL: The perspective of a design wall means that all areas of the quilt are relative to each other.

When reviewing a quilt that is on the floor or a horizontal flat surface, the perspective is not correct. The further bits become narrow and the closer bits enlarge.

TIME: Walking away and returning to a project often alerts you to issues or problems that might not be obvious in the flow of making. Allow for a bit of time between steps to let the project settle.

Time is most important toward the end of a project. Try not to rush to the finish. Enjoy each step as it appears, and the results will show the effort.

Organic Appliqué

CHAPTER 4
projects

58

69

77

86

101

110

117

125

arrival

TECHNIQUES

Broderie Perse

English paper piecing

Needle-turn appliqué

Hand quilting

Take your mind to the place where the Australian earth meets the sky: the horizon. It is near and far in the same glance and full of open spaces. Leaves are drawn long and skinny. Clouds give the feeling of moving open air. Windmills imply a gentle use of the earth's energy. The effect of a side border is created from appliquéd English paper-pieced blocks in a combination of a graphic plaid and a soft stripe. I chose Kaffe Fassett shot cotton backgrounds because the weave of two colors gives the background a bit of a lift and connection to the colors.

The print fabrics include birds and leaves that are cut in a Broderie Perse style. The ones I used were from my Horizons fabric collection for FreeSpirit Fabrics. Your prints will add your own style to the project. I liked the play of plaids for the boats. In some cases, I chose colors based on the literal color of the object, but in others I gave no regard for the natural color.

MATERIALS

Yardage is based on 42˝ width of fabric unless otherwise noted. The shot cottons used for the background of this quilt were a bit wider.

ASSORTED SHOT COTTONS: ⅔ yard (65 cm) of 2 fabrics and ⅓ yard (30 cm) of 1 fabric for 5 strips for backgrounds

ASSORTED PLAIDS AND STRIPES: ¼ yard (25 cm) *each* of 6 different prints for English paper-pieced blocks

CIRCULAR PRINT: Scraps at least 4˝ × 4˝ (10 cm × 10 cm) *or* enough yardage to fussy cut 5 motifs for centers of English paper-pieced blocks

ASSORTED PRINTS: 1 fat quarter for each of the following:

• Boab trees

• Emus, birds, dingo

SCRAPS: 2 prints for bias landscape shapes, plus more scraps for boats, sails, rocks, circles, clouds, leaves, waves, and stars

PRINTS WITH LARGE BIRDS, LEAVES, AND WINDMILLS: Fat quarters *or* ⅓ yard (30 cm) *or* as much as necessary to cut a bird, leaves, and windmills for the Broderie Perse shapes (You can choose as many prints as you like to add your chosen elements. I used the Magpie, Gum Leaf, and Wind Power prints from my Horizons collection for FreeSpirit Fabrics.)

BACKING: 3 yards (2.75 m)

BATTING: 52˝ × 60˝ (135 cm × 155 cm)

BINDING: ½ yard (50 cm)

PAPER PIECES AND ACRYLIC TEMPLATES FOR THE MRS. PEACH BLOCK, LARGE SIZE: Enough to make 5 blocks (*optional*)

APPLIQUÉ SUPPLIES, including Wash-Away Appliqué Sheets

VARIEGATED QUILTING THREADS: 3 different spools of Eleganza perle cotton #8

CUTTING

Assorted shot cottons

- From the background fabrics, cut a total of 5 strips, each 11″ × width of fabric. These are oversized; you will trim them to 10¾″ after appliqué for a finished strip height of 10¼″.

Assorted plaids and stripes

- Use the Mrs. Peach commercial paper pieces as a guide or make your own from the patterns (page 65). Cut the shapes, adding a ¼″ seam allowance (or if you have the acrylic cutting templates, use them and do not add the seam allowance). I did not use the 8 small triangles that would connect the spokes.

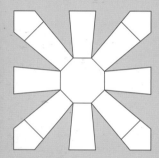

The Mrs. Peach templates are designed by Marg George and are available as commercially cut papers. Or see the patterns (page 65).

PLAID A: Cut 12 spokes and 12 corners.

STRIPE A: Cut 12 spokes.

PLAIDS B AND C: Cut 4 spokes and 4 corners from each.

STRIPES B AND C: Cut 4 spokes from each.

CIRCLE PRINT A: Cut 3 octagons (optional fussy cutting).

CIRCLE PRINTS B AND C: Cut 1 octagon from each.

NOTE

I made three Mrs. Peach blocks in one colorway and two in different colors. You can choose this arrangement or create one of your own.

Making the Quilt

MRS. PEACH BLOCKS

1. Lay out 1 set of the paper shapes to set the pattern and avoid confusion.

2. Use the paper to trace the shapes onto the wrong side of the fabric and cut away, including a ¼″ seam allowance.

3. Position the paper within the traced lines. Run a glue stick around the edge of the papers. Fold the edges of the fabric over and finger-press in place. Place them back into formation as you go.

4. Join the corners to the 4 striped spokes. Join the spokes to the octagon, alternating flat and corner spokes to make the square.

5. Spray with Best Press and then press with a hot iron to set the folded edges.

6. Arrange the blocks in alternating colors or a pattern that you like. Sew the adjoining corners and spokes from block to block to create a long piece. Set aside to be appliquéd later.

APPLIQUÉ

Refer to Needle-Turn Appliqué (page 34) for instructions on preparing appliqué shapes, basting, and stitching.

1. Prepare each background strip by marking the finished size with a chalk pencil so that you don't go over into the seam allowance. Zigzag or serge the edges to avoid fraying.

2. Select your appliqué fabrics, prepare the appliqué shapes, and arrange them as desired. You can use the shapes provided (pages 66–68), but feel free to decorate your world as you see it!

Consider these shapes:

- **3 BOATS (1 WITH A SAIL):** Look for fabrics with a texture that might be imagined as wood. For the sail, use something light and airy. The masts should be dark and about ¼″ finished. I used the bias method but on the straight grain and made 1 long piece that I then cut into short pieces:

3 masts 4″–6″

3 masts 3″

3 masts 4″

- **3 WAVES (4″–7″ LONG):** These help create a sense of place. To draw them, use smooth wavy lines—think mustaches! I included a pattern (page 67) to get you started.

- **4 LONG CLOUDS (4″–9″ LONG) IN GRAY:** The size isn't important; you just want to suggest clouds in the sky. Modify the wave pattern or draw your own.

- **3 STARS:** Of course, they are yellow and shining bright in the sky.

- **3 BOAB TREES:** The boab trees were made with dark leafy fabrics.

- **3 EMU:** Mine were made with small repetitive prints, but you can use your imagination and find feather-textured prints. Aboriginal prints would be great!

- **1 DINGO:** I made it with stripes, naturally.

- **4 LAND LINES:** These simply provide a horizon to create a sense of earth. They are about 16″–26″ in length and made using the bias method (page 36), so they are purposefully irregular.

- **2 RED ROCKS:** Australia is famous for its red earth, so the 2 red rocks had to be included! They are about 6″ wide and 2″ high. I included 1 pattern but draw your own shapes to make them different.

- **3 WINDMILLS:** These are fussy cut from my Horizons collection but could be made using a circle print fabric and a triangle. The pattern (page 67) is included.

- **BRODERIE PERSE MOTIFS:** I chose 6 leaves, 3 magpies, and 3 windmills.

- **CIRCLES (2¼″–3″ DIAMETER):** These circles gently reference the aboriginal dot art using circles. The sprinkling of the circles adds a bit of interest in the open spaces.

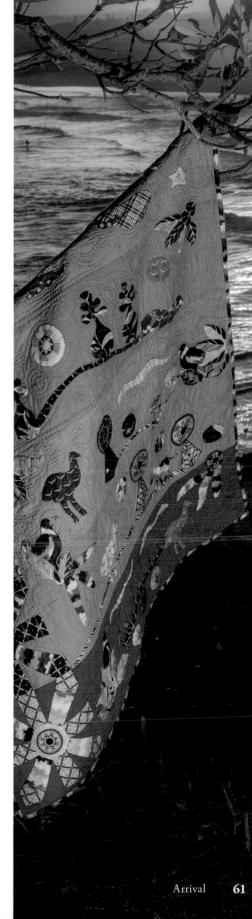

3. This is a good time to use the design wall. Position the background fabrics in place. Pin the paper-pieced blocks to the left-hand side. Arrange the shapes on each strip until you are happy with the layout.

4. When you are happy with the layout, pin or baste the shapes in place.

5. Appliqué each strip separately.

6. Use Eleganza perle cotton #8 to stitch the lettering *They came by boat …* (page 65) onto the last panel on the bottom panel.

7. When you have completed the appliqué, trim each strip to 10¾″. Join them together along the width. It is possible now to add a few motifs that go over the seam joins. I added some of Broderie Perse after the backgrounds were sewn together.

8. Reposition the Mrs. Peach blocks, aligning the joins between the blocks with the seams. Remove the papers and pin or baste in place. Appliqué in place.

composition

Here is where you can stop and think about the project—much easier now than after all the appliqué is done! Use the design wall, step back or take a photo, and assess the composition. Really look at the quilt and consider:

CONTRAST: Do all the shapes show up on the background?

HARMONY: Do all of the strips work independently and then together?

SCALE AND PROPORTION: Is there a balance to the size and placement of shapes throughout the quilt?

You may want to add more or position shapes differently, which is perfectly okay.

Quilt assembly

Quilting

Arrival is hand quilted using perle cotton #8 variegated threads. Quilt around the appliqué shapes first. The background stitching follows swirling, curvy randomly drawn lines made using a chalk pencil. They are indicative of the shape of blowing wind … in my mind, anyway. I wanted to loosely fill the background space. You might also consider horizontal stitching, which could bring to mind the idea of a horizon line.

Swirling quilting lines fill the space and add to the story.

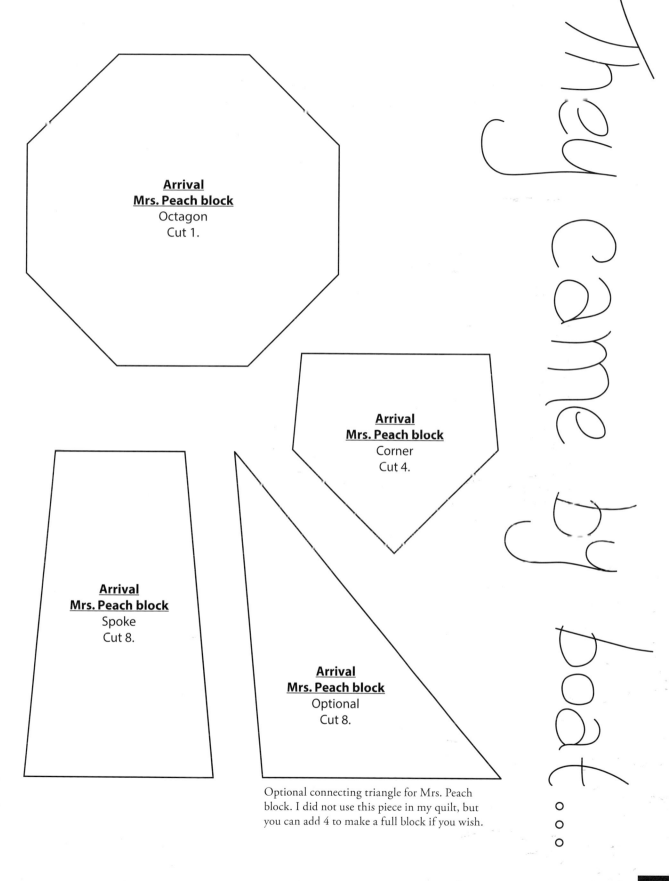

Arrival
Mrs. Peach block
Octagon
Cut 1.

Arrival
Mrs. Peach block
Corner
Cut 4.

Arrival
Mrs. Peach block
Spoke
Cut 8.

Arrival
Mrs. Peach block
Optional
Cut 8.

Optional connecting triangle for Mrs. Peach block. I did not use this piece in my quilt, but you can add 4 to make a full block if you wish.

They came by boat...

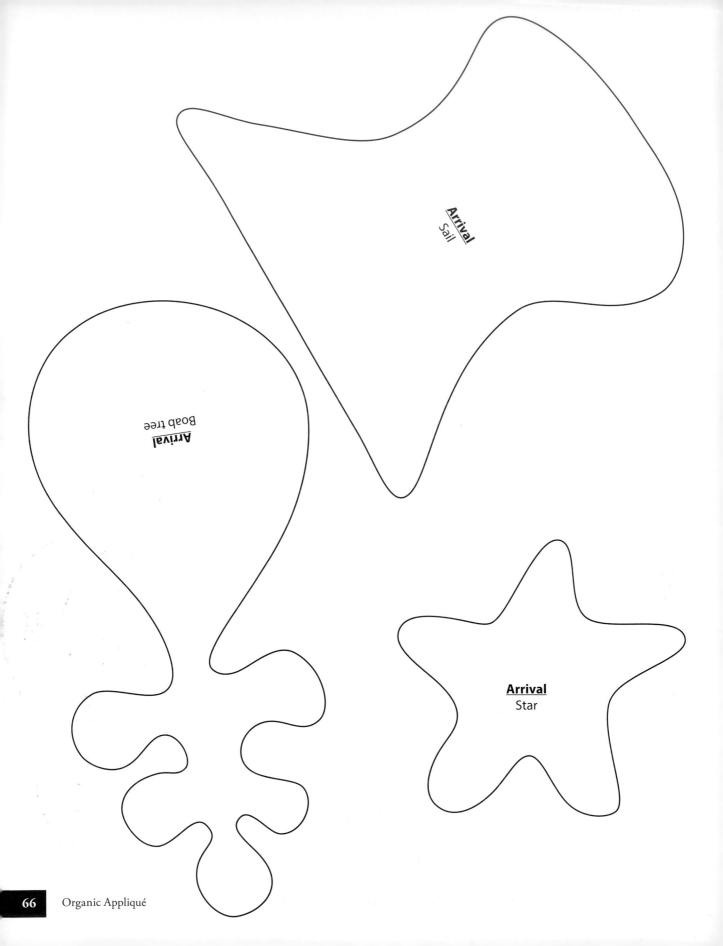

Arrival
Sail

Arrival
Boab tree

Arrival
Star

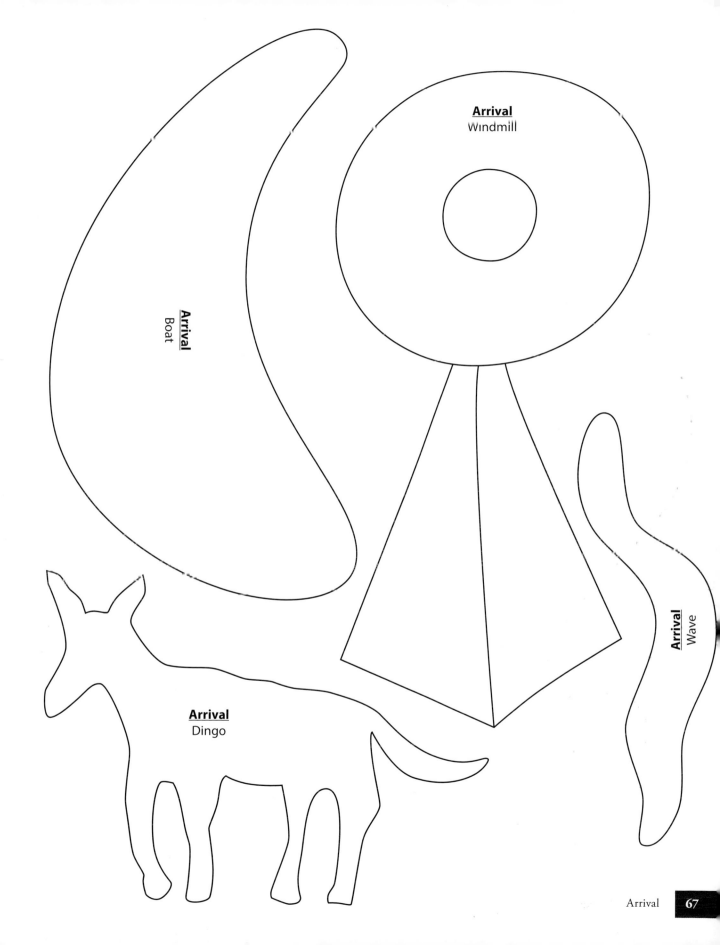

Arrival
Windmill

Arrival
Boat

Arrival
Wave

Arrival
Dingo

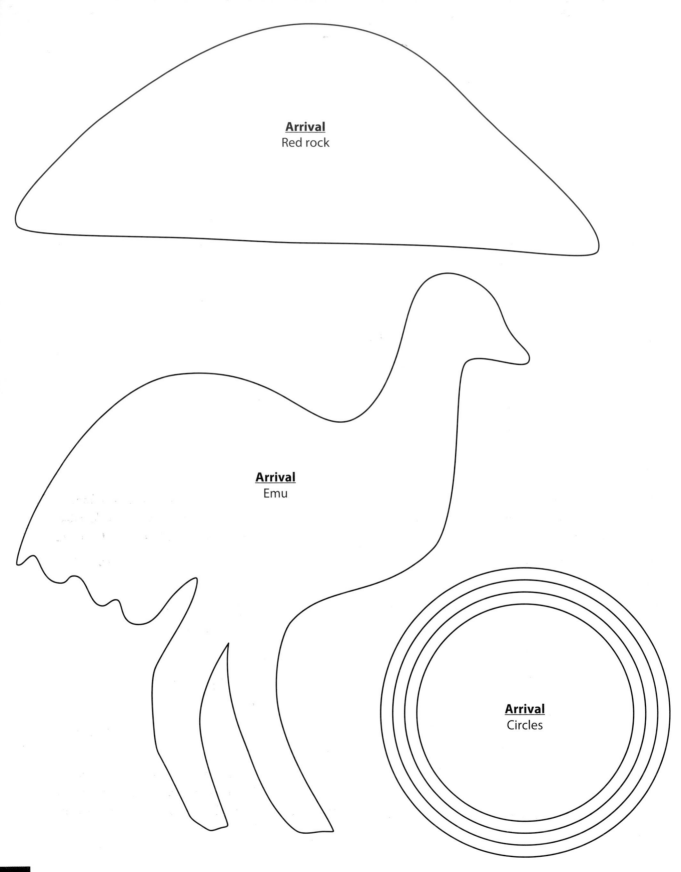

Arrival
Red rock

Arrival
Emu

Arrival
Circles

stolen moments

FINSHED QUILT: 44″ × 62″ (112 cm × 158 cm)

The lines in *Stolen Moments* reveal a simple still life of a boab tree hosting a flock of colorful birds. It has morphed many times from the original dream and has been made in moments stolen from a busy schedule, the creative energy stored up until time availed itself for making.

Australia can be a harsh country. Life bursts and then dries to a crisp. This design is a reference to my good friend in quilting, Cath Babidge, who fostered my love of this tree's shape and introduced me to Mary Jane Hannaford. Mary Jane found quilting later in life and made quilts for her family that were rich in references to her life. Birds, people, poems, and messages all had a place. Talk about off the grid—her quilts were totally unique and without common structure. The pieced lines made of rectangle scraps reference Mary Jane's quilts.

TECHNIQUES

Needle-turn appliqué

Piecing scrap strips

Bias strips

Hand quilting

MATERIALS

Yardage is based on 42″ width of fabric unless otherwise noted. The shot cottons used for the background of this quilt were a bit wider.

LINEN: 2 yards (1.85 m), at least 60″ wide (155 cm wide), for background

BROWN-AND-WHITE WAVY STRIPE: 1½ yards (1.4 m) for tree and branches

DARK GREEN PRINT: ⅓ yard (30 cm) for leaves

LIGHT GREEN PRINT: ⅓ yard (30 cm) for leaves

ASSORTED PRINTS AND STRIPES: ⅓ yard (30 cm) of 1–3 fabrics for 7 birds

ORANGE PRINTS: ⅓ yard (30 cm) for orange leaves

BROWN GRAPHIC PRINT: ⅓ yard (30 cm) for stems

ASSORTED SCRAPS:

• A number of scrap fabrics to total ½ yard (0.5 m) for pieced dividing lines; you will need approximately

90 rectangles about 1¾″ × 4″. (Collect scraps from your stash that have a lot of variety. Select colors that are warm and cool, light and dark, saturated or faded.)

• A number of circular motif prints for 34 circles 3″ in diameter

• Butterfly motif for Broderie Perse

• 2 emu bodies and 4 emu legs

BACKING: 3 yards (2.75 m)

BATTING: 52″ × 70″ (135 cm × 180 cm)

BINDING: ½ yard (50 cm)

APPLIQUÉ SUPPLIES, including Wash-Away Appliqué Sheets

QUILTING THREADS: Eleganza perle cotton #8 (I used a variegated thread that was both darker and lighter than the background fabric. To outline the appliqué shapes, I used dark shades of the colors.)

CUTTING

Background

- Cut a rectangle a few inches bigger than the finished size of the quilt (44″ × 62″). (My starting piece was 48″ × 66″.) You will trim it after appliqué.

Pieced dividing lines

- Cut about 90 rectangles 1¾″ wide × approximately 4″. They can be a little longer or shorter for variety.

Appliqué prints

- See Appliqué (below) for instructions.

Making the Quilt

APPLIQUÉ

Refer to Needle-Turn Appliqué (page 34) for instructions on preparing appliqué shapes, basting, and stitching.

To make the pieced dividing lines, join the rectangles end to end along the 1¾″ sides to make a long strip about 9 yards (8.3 m) in length. Fold over a ¼″ seam on both sides and press flat. You will cut this into sections later.

Leaves

1. Cut the light-green and dark-green leaf fabrics each into 3 strips 4″ × width of fabric.

2. Join a light strip and a dark strip together along the length; repeat with the 4 remaining light and dark strips. Using the templates cut from the leaf patterns in varying sizes, cut out 17–20 leaves with the seam in the middle. This creates a side where the light hits and a side for shadow.

Birds

Cut viewing templates using the bird shape and fussy cut 6 or 7 birds.

Boab Tree

1. Cut out a bulbous shape from the brown-and-white wavy stripe fabric. Make it any shape you want!

2. Cut 3 yards (2.75 m) of bias stems for the branches.

Bushes

1. Cut 2 yards of bias stems for the bushes. Make them a bit wider than the boab tree branches.

2. From the orange fabrics, cut 5–7 large, 5–7 medium, and 5–7 small leaves for the bushes.

Large Circles

Cut 34 circles 3″ (2½″ finished). I used a Kaffe Fassett fabric with a variety of circular motifs and a fabric from my Horizons collection that had images of boabs and emus. I made 22 of the circles dark and 12 a consistent color (turquoise).

Emu

Using the *Arrival* emu pattern (page 68), cut 2 emu bodies with 2 legs each.

Small Circles

Cut 3 circles 1½″ for berries on the bushes.

Now for the fun part!

Layout

1. Position the background fabric on the design wall.

2. Gently mark a vertical chalk line through the center of the quilt top.

3. Measure the quilt into thirds horizontally and mark 2 chalk lines across the width.

4. Using the length of your arm and a smooth arc, draw a line from the first one-third mark on the left side to the top center mark. Repeat for the top right and both bottom corners.

5. Position and pin sections of the pieced lines along the drawn lines; then add the second and third sections of the pieced lines in each corner. Here's the thing: The placement of the arcs is not exact, and that is what gives the quilt its charm. The space between the arcs is approximately 6″ for the first section and 5″ for the second.

6. Add the remaining pieced strips in a straight line to connect the curved lines at each side.

Tip It always helps at this stage to take a photograph. Have a look at the photo to see if there are any areas that draw the eye more than others. If you have any doubts about any of the lines, adjust until you are happy.

The next step is to walk away for a while. When you return, have another look and consider if there is anything new in how you see your lines.

If you are a perfectionist, which I admittedly am *not*, you can measure from your first arc and make marks so that your arcs are parallel. This is not hard to do. Follow the marks with your pieced lines, pin, and then baste in place.

PUTTING IT TOGETHER

1. Appliqué the pieced dividing lines.

2. Position your appliqué shapes on the background in the middle of the quilt. Start with the base of the boab tree. When you are happy with that, add the branches, the leaves, and finally the birds and butterfly.

3. Position the stems and branches of the bushes. Add the leaves and a few circles.

4. Take a photo and review the placement of the appliqué. When you are happy, pin or baste and then stitch in place. I find that when working with big shapes like this, it is a good idea to pin and then baste the shapes in place. The large background area means that a good amount of fabric will be scrunched in your hands, so not having any pins to worry about is a big bonus!

5. When the basted appliqué is complete, position the circles, referring to the quilt photograph. I put an odd number of circles in each of the arcs and alternated dark circles with turquoise circles.

6. Appliqué the circles in place.

7. Add the emus in the top corners and appliqué.

Quilting

This quilt is hand quilted using Eleganza perle cotton #8. I chose a variegated color that was both lighter and darker than the backgrounds. I also used dark shades of the colors to outline the appliqué shapes.

1. To start, stitch around each of the appliqué shapes and all the pieced lines. Always start in the middle of the quilt and work around. These stitches will make the appliqué stand out and also add more basting security to the quilt.

2. For the background area, use a chalk pencil and a straight-edge ruler to draw straight lines ½″–¾″ apart. Start at the middle of the top and fill the background spaces. When there are a few lines in place, it is easy to keep adding lines.

3. To quilt the background, it helps to thread and run 2–3 needles at a time. Fill the space in the hoop with stitches before moving down the quilt. Although it appears like a lot of quilting, it was possible to complete this quilt in a few weeks—and I might add in the heat of the summer for me!

Quilt assembly

Organic Appliqué

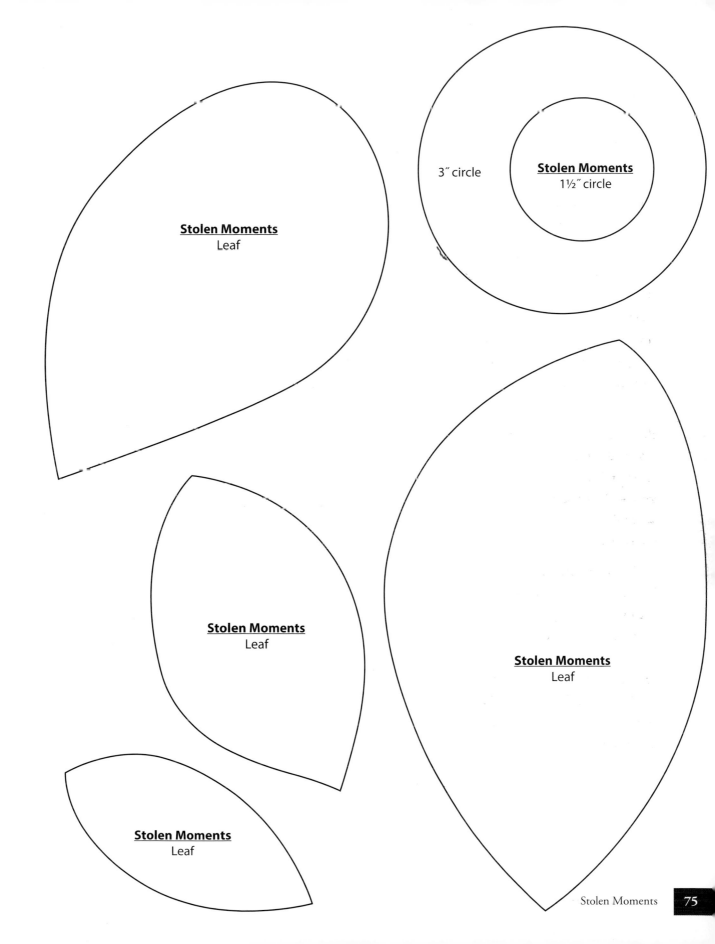

Stolen Moments
Leaf

3˝ circle

Stolen Moments
1½˝ circle

Stolen Moments
Leaf

Stolen Moments
Leaf

Stolen Moments
Leaf

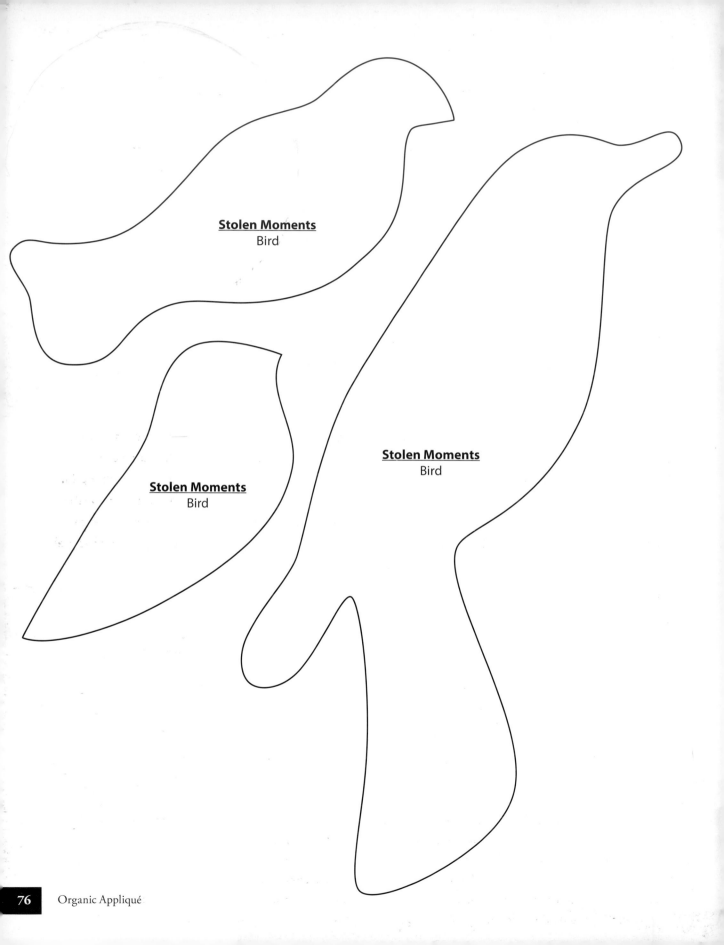

Stolen Moments
Bird

Stolen Moments
Bird

Stolen Moments
Bird

surrounding stars

If, at the start of this project, I had focused on how long it would take, I never would have started it. However, a hand-piecing project is fantastic for the pick-up-and-go times. I have loved grabbing it over the years and watching it progress slowly over time. Having said that, there was nothing better than realizing it was ready to be built into a quilt. Great satisfaction was achieved!

Liberty Fabrics are perfect for hand piecing. The beauty of each print stands the test of time as a classic print. Their beauty lasts a lifetime, and many of the prints are decades old as proof. I added in a gray stripe with extra diamonds to give an alternating visual pattern.

TECHNIQUES

English paper piecing

Appliqué

Adding borders

Mitered corners

Some fabrics beg to be used in large spaces, and a large border on a quilt can be a simple but effective way to finish off a design. I like prints that run along the length of the quilt, and when they can be cut in four long strips, even better. It was a no-brainer to use Anna Maria Horner's beautiful Social Climber print for FreeSpirit Fabrics to frame this quilt. I considered mitered corners, but when I auditioned them on the design wall, it was clear that this fabric didn't need the extra effort. Instead, the borders wrap around the quilt, allowing the pattern to do its magic. The border fabrics make a nice frame that is simple but effective!

MATERIALS

Yardage is based on 42" width of fabric unless otherwise noted.

ASSORTED PRINTS FOR STAR CENTER DIAMONDS: ⅛ yard (10 cm) *each* of 27 different prints (You will need more fabric if fussy cutting the diamonds.)

ASSORTED PRINTS FOR STAR SURROUNDS: ⅛ yard (10 cm) WOF of 27 different prints *or* more of the same prints used for the centers (more if fussy cutting)

STRIPE FABRIC: 1¼ yard (1.15 m) for diamonds surrounding Marg's Star block

BACKGROUND: 1½ yards (1.4 m) for paper-pieced hexagons and background frame

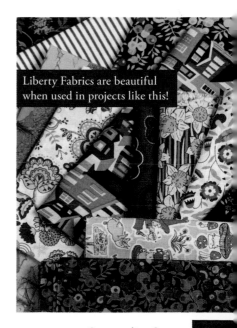

Liberty Fabrics are beautiful when used in projects like this!

NOTE

The background of my paper-pieced center is Liberty Fabric's cotton Tana lawn, which is a bit more expensive than most regular cottons but also wider. To save fabric, I chose to appliqué the paper-pieced center onto a background frame with mitered corners. It would be easy to appliqué the entire pieced section onto a solid piece of fabric instead. If you would rather use this option, buy 2½ yards of fabric total.

Surrounding Stars

INNER BORDER: 1⅞ yards (1.8 m)

OUTER BORDER: 2¼ yards (2.1 m)

BACKING: 5 yards (4.6 m)

BATTING: 82″ × 88″ (210 cm × 225 cm)

BINDING: ¾ yard (70 cm)

ENGLISH PAPER-PIECING PRECUT PAPERS: Buy the following precut papers, or make your own from the patterns (page 84):

• 1″ MARG'S STARS BY MARGARET SAMPSON-GEORGE PRECUT PAPERS: 3–4 packs. (1 pack makes 8 stars, so buy 4 packs if you want enough pieces to make all the stars without reusing the papers.) These papers are commercially available from paperpieces.com or Imprezzio Cutting & Engraving.

1″ HEXAGONS: 1 pack of 100 pieces

1″ DIAMONDS (FOR OUTER STRIPED DIAMONDS): 3 packs of 100 each

2″ DIAMONDS (FOR BORDER STARS): 1 pack *or* 24 pieces

• 1″ MARG'S STAR ACRYLIC CUTTING TEMPLATES (*optional*)

APPLIQUÉ SUPPLIES

VARIEGATED QUILTING THREADS: 3 different spools of Eleganza perle cotton #8

CUTTING

To prepare your shapes, you may want to cut all of your fabrics first or cut them a block at a time. You will need to make 23 full stars and 4 half-stars.

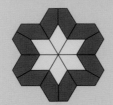

Marg's Star block, designed by Margaret Sampson-George

Here, Marg's Star block is surrounded by striped diamonds and background hexagons.

Assorted prints

For each Marg's Star block, cut the following:

• **CENTER STAR:** 6 diamonds from 1 fabric

• **CENTER STAR SURROUND:** 12 partial hexagons from 1 fabric—6 slanted to the right and 6 slanted to the left

Stripe fabric

• Cut 12 diamonds 1″ for each full star and 6 diamonds for each half-star (300 total). I oriented my stripe along the length of the diamond.

Background

• Cut 98 hexagons 1″.

• Cut 2 strips 4″ × 34½″ for the background frame top and bottom.

• Cut 2 strips 4″ × 40½″ for the background frame sides.

• *Optional:* Instead of cutting and assembling a background frame, cut a rectangle 34½″ × 40½″ and appliqué the English paper-pieced quilt center to it. See the note in Materials (page 77).

Inner border stars

• For each star, cut 6 diamonds 2″ (24 total) from assorted fabrics.

Inner border

• Cut 2 strips 10½″ × 34½″ for the top and bottom borders.

• Cut 2 strips 10½″ × 60½″ for the side borders.

Outer border

• Cut 1 strip 10½″ × 60½″ for the right side border.

• Cut 1 strip 10½″ × 64½″ for the bottom border.

• Cut 1 strip 10½″ × 70½″ for the left side border.

• Cut 1 strip 10½″ × 74½″ for the top border.

NOTE

There are only 98 full hexagons cut from the background fabric because all 4 sides of the English paper-pieced center section are actually appliquéd onto the assembled background fabric, so they do not need to be filled to a straight edge.

Make the Quilt

MARG'S STAR BLOCKS

1. Prepare the paper pieces. See English Paper Piecing (page 43) for detailed instructions.

2. Whipstitch each Marg's Star block together in the following order to make 23 full stars.

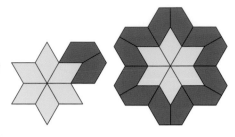

- Stitch 6 diamonds, joined in 2 halves, to make a star center.

- Join partial hexagons to the right and left side of each star point diamond; then join to adjacent partial hexagons.

- Make V's with 2 striped diamonds.

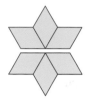

- Join the striped V's between the angled sides of the partial hexagons.

3. Make 4 half-stars, following the same process as Step 2.

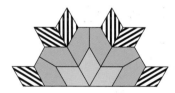

4. Join 12 background hexagons to 4 of the full stars. You may want to refer to the center assembly diagram (next page) and lay out the stars first to choose which stars to use in these positions.

QUILT CENTER ASSEMBLY

English Paper Pieced Center

1. Referring to the center assembly diagram (next page), arrange the full stars without background hexagons into 3 columns of 5 stars each, leaving space for another column between them.

2. Nestle 2 columns of 4 stars each into the open spaces, starting with a star with the added background hexagons and alternating between the stars with and stars without added hexagons.

3. Fill in the joins with background hexagons.

Remember that you do not need to add hexagons to the spaces on all 4 sides of the center because you will appliqué the outer edges of the side stars to the background fabric frame.

4. Hand stitch all the stars and added hexagons together.

5. When the stars are joined together, remove the papers from the middle stars, leaving the papers in place on the outside edges. Spray the edge shapes with Best Press and press to secure the finished edge. It is best to leave the outer papers in until you are ready to appliqué the outer edges in place.

Center assembly

Make the Background Frame

1. With the right sides up, arrange the 4 background fabric strips on the design wall. The ends should overlap just enough to cover the adjacent corner.

2. At each corner, fold the horizontal background strip under itself so that it meets the edge of the adjacent strip and forms a 45° angle. Pin the fold in place and press.

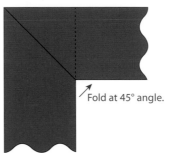

Fold at 45° angle.

3. Stitch the seamline that you have pressed. Or you can appliqué the mitered seam together by hand.

Background frame

QUILT ASSEMBLY

1. Position the 2″ diamond stars at the center of the inner border strips. Press and remove the papers; then appliqué the stars in place.

2. Position the English paper-pieced center over the background frame. Pin in place. Carefully remove the outer papers and baste in place.

3. Appliqué the outer edge to the frame.

4. Join the top and bottom inner borders to the quilt center, matching and pinning the center and ends. Repeat for the sides.

5. Join the right side border in the same method. Repeat for the bottom border and then the left side. Add the final border at the top.

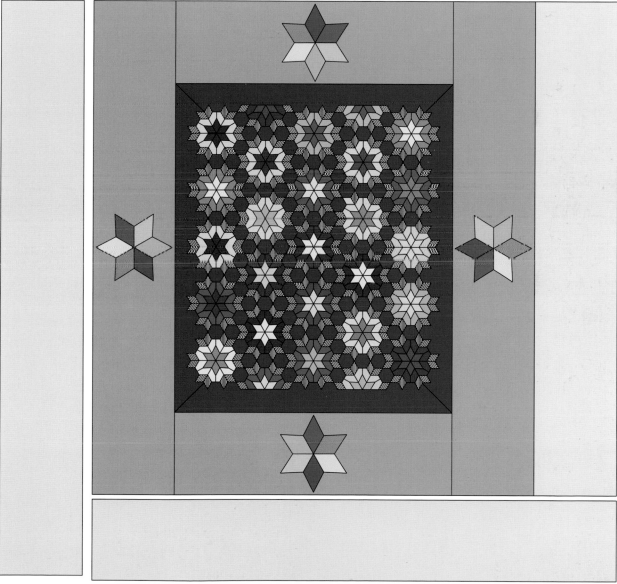

Quilt assembly

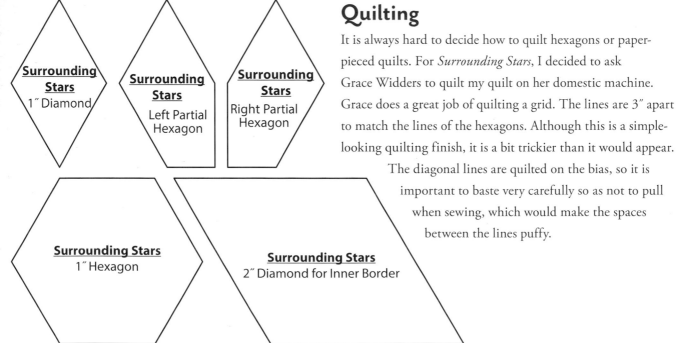

Surrounding Stars
1˝ Diamond

Surrounding Stars
Left Partial Hexagon

Surrounding Stars
Right Partial Hexagon

Surrounding Stars
1˝ Hexagon

Surrounding Stars
2˝ Diamond for Inner Border

Quilting

It is always hard to decide how to quilt hexagons or paper-pieced quilts. For *Surrounding Stars*, I decided to ask Grace Widders to quilt my quilt on her domestic machine. Grace does a great job of quilting a grid. The lines are 3˝ apart to match the lines of the hexagons. Although this is a simple-looking quilting finish, it is a bit trickier than it would appear.

The diagonal lines are quilted on the bias, so it is important to baste very carefully so as not to pull when sewing, which would make the spaces between the lines puffy.

folk art heart

FINISHED QUILT: 67˝ × 67˝ (170 cm × 170 cm)

TECHNIQUES

Needle-turn appliqué

Sew-in or appliqué circles

Piecing

Most of my quilts are made using saturated colors. In this case, the fabric was from a precut 10˝ square of Gardenvale by Jen Kingwell Designs for Moda. The colors are softer than I normally use, which was perfect for the folk art children's theme I was designing. The trick for me was to add a bit of graphic integrity with the red-and-white stripe and the addition of black. That one dark fabric used sparingly added just enough interest. Without these elements, it might not have enough contrast. The border also adds a lot of interest. There is a balance with crisp diagonal lines and soft curves throughout the quilt.

I have instructed here to inset piece the circles, but if you are falling in love with appliqué, it is also possible to needle turn the circles!

For a project like this, I like to gather images of things that relate to the theme before committing to the designs.

MATERIALS

Yardage is based on 42˝ width of fabric unless otherwise noted.

ASSORTED 10˝ × 10˝ SQUARES: 60 or more (such as 2 Moda Layer Cakes) *or* an assortment of scraps to total approximately 5½ yards

BLACK-AND-WHITE SHIRTING: 1⅓ yards (1.2 m)

RED-AND-WHITE STRIPE: 1⅓ yards (1.2 m)

BLACK SOLID: ¾ yard (70 cm)

DARK SPOT: ¾ yard (70 cm)

CIRCLE TEMPLATES: 7˝, 7½˝, 8˝, and 8½˝ (or use a rotary circle cutter)

BACKING: 4½ yards (4.2 m)

BATTING: 75˝ × 75˝ (190 cm × 190 cm)

BINDING: ⅝ yard (60 cm)

APPLIQUÉ SUPPLIES

QUILTING THREADS: 2–3 spools of white perle cotton #12

CUTTING

Assorted 10˝ × 10˝ squares

- See Making the Quilt (at right) to cut the pieces as you make the blocks.

Black-and-white shirting

- Cut a 20½˝ × 20½˝ square for the medallion background.

- Cut 2 strips 3¼ × width of fabric and subcut 24 squares 3¼˝ × 3¼˝. Cut these squares in half diagonally to make 48 half-square triangles for the corners of the Kaleido Triangle blocks. Set aside these triangles and the remainder of this fabric to make the Kaleido Triangle blocks in the fourth border.

Red-and-white stripe

- Cut 2 strips 4˝ × width of fabric. Use a template made from pattern B to cut 24 curved outer triangles for the medallion center.

- Cut 4 strips 1½˝ × 19½˝ for the first border.

- Cut 4 strips 1½˝ × 38½˝ for the third border.

- Cut 4 strips 4½˝ × width of fabric. Use a template made from pattern C to cut 68 triangles and 4 half-triangles for the outer pieced border.

Black solid

- Cut 2 strips 4˝ × width of fabric. Use a template made from pattern A to cut 20 curved inner triangles and pattern Half A to cut 4 half-triangles and 4 reversed half-triangles for the medallion center.

- Cut 8 squares 1½˝ × 1½˝ for the first and third borders.

- Cut 4 squares 4½˝ × 4½˝ for the outer pieced border.

- Cut 6 strips 2˝ × WOF. Join end to end and subcut:

  2 strips 56½˝

  2 strips 59½˝

Dark spot

- Cut 4 strips 4½˝ × width of fabric. Use a template made from pattern C to cut 68 triangles and 4 half-triangles for the outer pieced border.

Making the Quilt

Refer to Needle-Turn Appliqué (page 34) for instructions on preparing appliqué shapes, basting, and stitching. For detailed instructions on sewing borders to a quilt, see Adding Borders (page 46). Refer to the quilt assembly diagram (page 93) for the following blocks and borders.

CENTER MEDALLION

FINISHED SIZE: 21˝ square

Curved Triangle Corners

1. Join the curved triangles A and B in a set of 6 stripe triangles and 5 black triangles for each of the 4 corners. The outside pieces are the half A and half A reversed triangles. Or you can join a full A triangle to each end and trim square.

2. Use the quarter-circle template E and cut 4 quarter-circles from the 10˝ squares. Fold in half to find the center of the pieced section and the center of the curved edge of the quarter-circle. Align and pin; then sew to join.

Medallion Appliqué and Assembly

1. Fold the medallion background in half both horizontally and vertically; mark the folded edges.

2. Mark chalk lines ½˝ in from each edge of the square. Position the 4 pieced corners along the lines and pin in place. Needle turn the curved edges to the background. The space between the half-circles is about 2½˝.

3. Trim away the background behind the corners.

4. Use the appliqué patterns (pages 94–100) to prepare the appliqué pieces for the center and the corners; appliqué in place.

5. Square up the completed medallion center to 19½˝ × 19½˝.

Medallion Border

1. Join a 19½″ red-stripe strip to opposite sides of the center medallion.

2. Join a 1½″ black square to each end of the remaining 19½″ red-stripe strips. Pin and sew to the other sides of the medallion.

APPLIQUÉ CIRCLE AND CHAIN LINK BORDER

Appliqué Circle Blocks

FINISHED BLOCK: 8½″ × 8½″

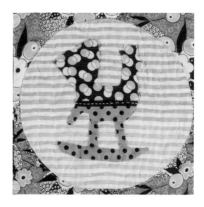

Tip When machine piecing the circles into the squares, it's easier if you keep the grain aligned the same for both shapes.

1. Choose 8 squares 10″ × 10″ to use for the block backgrounds. Fold the squares in half vertically and horizontally; press to mark. Use a 7½″ circle template to cut a circle out of the middle of each square.

2. Use an 8½″ circle template to cut circles from 8 additional 10″ squares for appliqué.

3. Select your appliqué fabrics, prepare the shapes, and arrange them on the 8½″ circles. Pin the shapes onto the circles with appliqué pins and needle turn in place.

4. Fold and press the appliquéd circles in half vertically and horizontally. Use the press marks to match and pin each circle into the cut-out center circle of a 10″ block background square. Sew the circles into the squares. Check after sewing to be sure there are no tucks or gathers in the seam.

5. Press the blocks flat and trim to 9″ × 9″ to square up.

NOTE

The instructions are for inset sewing the circles into the squares, but it is just as much fun to appliqué the circles. To appliqué, don't cut the circle out of the center of each square in Step 1 (at left). Make an 8″ card stock circle, the finished size of the circle. Run a basting stitch around the edge of the 8½″ fabric circle. Place the circle right side down, with the card stock template on top, so that you can see the stitches. Pull the thread until the circle is enclosed. Knot the thread. Press; then remove the template. Pin and appliqué in place.

Chain Link Blocks

FINISHED BLOCK: 6¼″ × 8½″

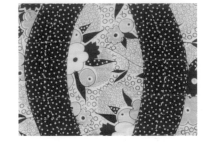

1. Prepare appliqué shapes using a template made from pattern D. For each block, cut 2 mirror shapes from a 10″ × 10″ square.

2. Cut 8 rectangles 6¾″ × 9″.

3. Fold a rectangle in half along the length and finger-press a center crease.

4. Position the 2 opposing chain links equal distance from the crease.

5. Pin and then appliqué in place.

6. Repeat Steps 3–5 to make 8 blocks total.

Appliqué Circle and Chain Link Border Assembly

1. Lay out the blocks around the center medallion, with the circle appliqué blocks in each corner alternating with the Chain Link blocks.

2. Sew the side borders together and join to the quilt.

3. Sew the top and bottom borders together and join to the quilt.

4. Use the 38½″ red-stripe strips and 4 black squares 1½″ × 1½″ to add the narrow third border, following the same process as the first border.

CIRCLE AND KALEIDO BORDER

Cut pieces from the assorted 10″ × 10″ squares.

Circle Blocks

FINISHED BLOCK: 8″ × 8″

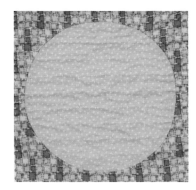

1. Refer to Appliqué Circle Blocks (page 89) to make 12 inset Circle blocks, but this time cut the circles to be inset 8″ in diameter and cut a 7″ centered circle from each of the background squares.

2. After pressing, square up the blocks to 8½″ × 8½″.

Kaleido Blocks

NOTE: *You will need 12 blocks made with 8 large C triangles each for a total of 96 C triangles, in addition to the 48 corner half-square triangles previously cut.*

These blocks vary slightly. Some are made from strip-pieced fabric and some are made with whole triangles. To have a nice mixture, follow these steps:

1. Use a variety of fabrics or scraps and cut strips that are 4½″ wide. Cut 48 C triangles from the print fabrics.

2. For additional variety, cut contrasting strips 2½″ wide and just long enough to cut at least 2 C triangles per strip from the remaining shirting fabric and any of the prints from the collection. Join along the length and cut an additional 48 C triangles.

3. Join the C triangles in pairs. Make 4 sets of matching pairs per block.

4. Join 2 pairs into halves. Match and pin 2 halves at the center to join them into an octagon.

5. Fold the outer edges of 4 opposing triangles in the octagon in half, and crease to mark the center. Fold and crease the half-square triangles in half along the long bias edge, being mindful not to stretch them.

6. Match the folds, pin, and then sew on 4 corner triangles to make the octagon a square.

7. Repeat Steps 4–6 to make 12 blocks total.

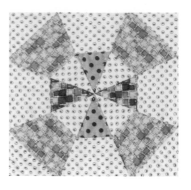

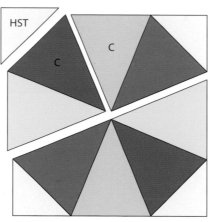

Kaleido block assembly. Note that a Kaleido block is made of 8 triangles that have 1 short straight edge and 2 long bias edges. When joined, they form an octagon.

Circle and Kaleido Border Assembly

1. Position the blocks around the outside of the quilt center, alternating the Circle blocks with the Kaleido blocks.

2. Sew the 5 side blocks together into borders and join to each side.

3. Repeat with the 7-block strips for the top and bottom borders.

4. Add the solid black side borders and then the top and bottom borders.

TRIANGLE BORDER

1. Referring to the quilt assembly diagram for color placement, lay out the dark spot and red-and-white stripe C triangles into 4 strips that have 17 full triangles and 1 half-triangle in each color.

2. Sew the triangles together to make 4 border strips.

3. Join a triangle border to the top and bottom of the quilt.

4. Join a 4½″ × 4½″ black square to each end of the 2 remaining triangle borders. Join the borders to the sides of the quilt.

Quilting

This quilt is hand quilted using perle cotton #12 in white. Quilt around the appliqué and along the seamlines of the blocks to stabilize the quilt. It is always a good idea to quilt around appliqué shapes to make them pop up a bit in the quilt. I had some help from my friend Helena Fooij to finish quilting this one in time!

Quilt assembly

Folk Art Heart
Heart

Folk Art Heart
Bird Wing

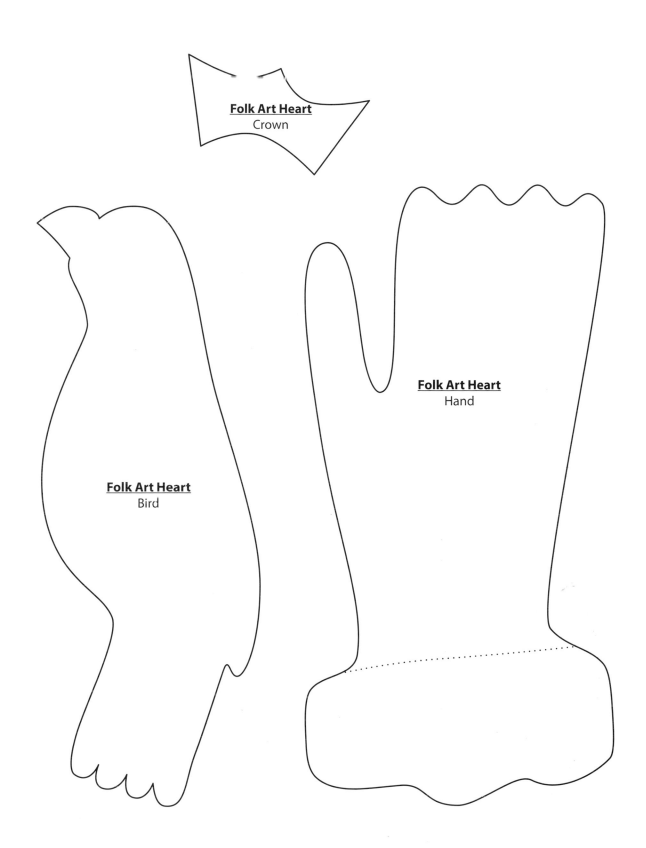

Folk Art Heart
Crown

Folk Art Heart
Hand

Folk Art Heart
Bird

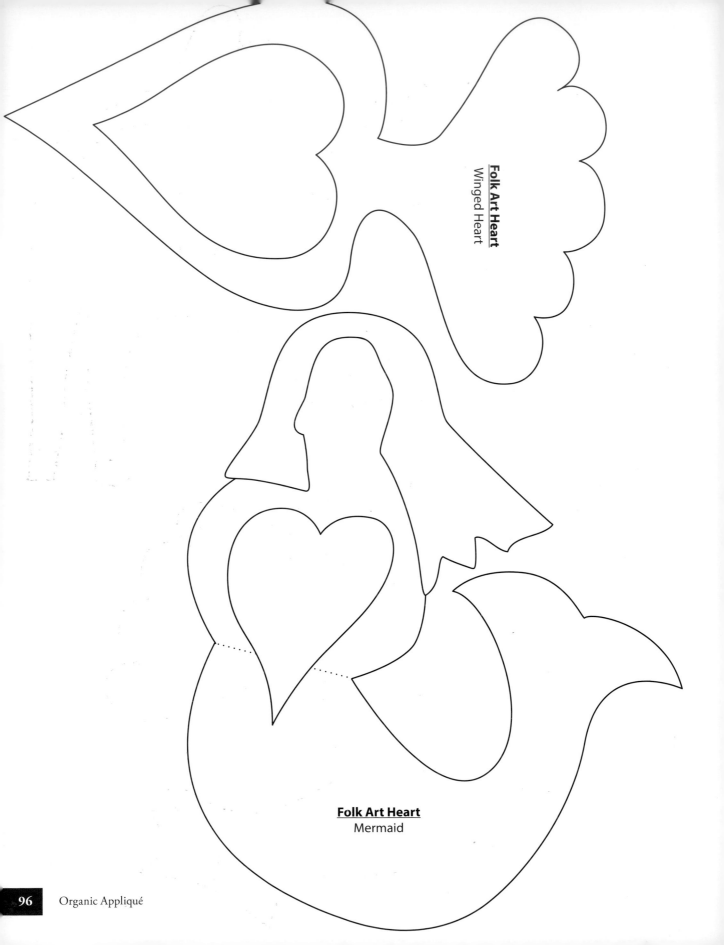

Folk Art Heart
Winged Heart

Folk Art Heart
Mermaid

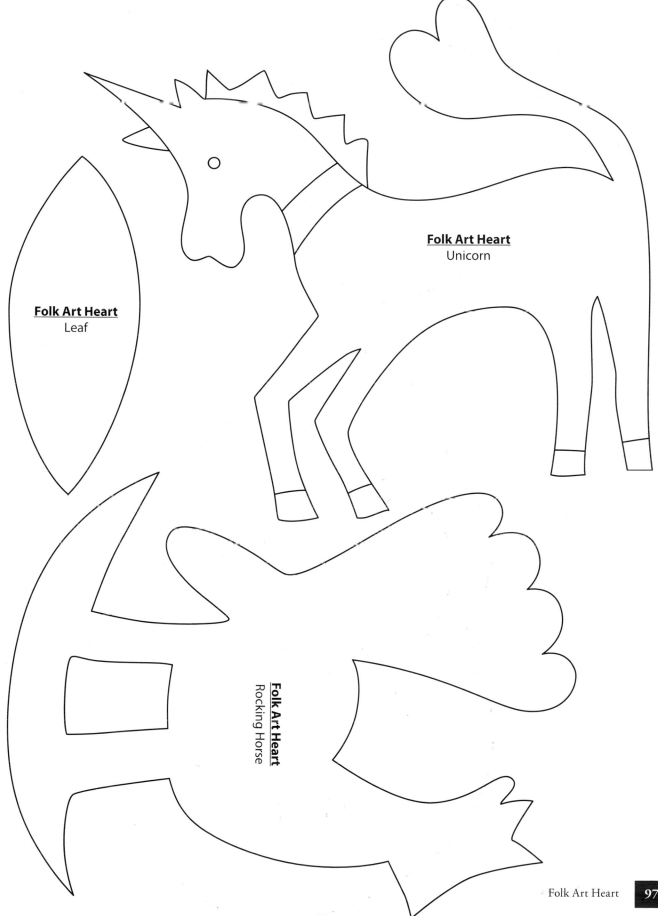

Folk Art Heart
Unicorn

Folk Art Heart
Leaf

Folk Art Heart
Rocking Horse

Folk Art Heart

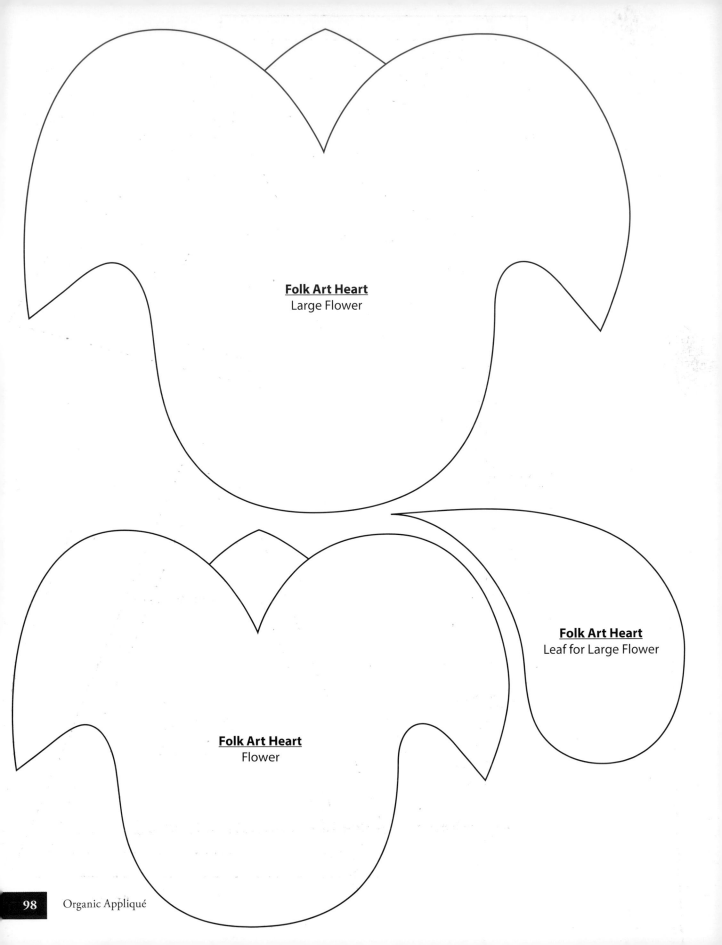

Folk Art Heart
Large Flower

Folk Art Heart
Leaf for Large Flower

Folk Art Heart
Flower

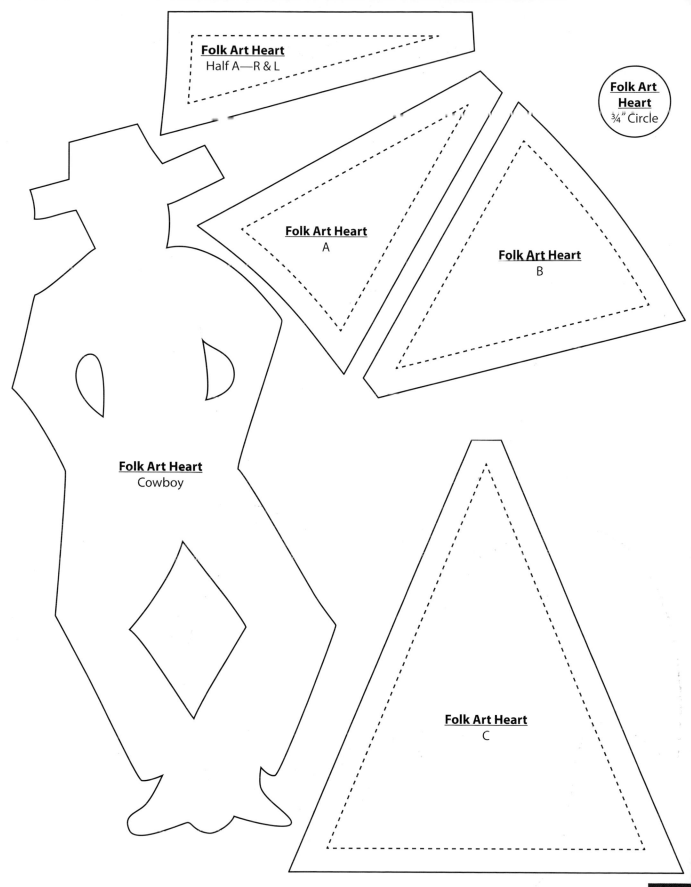

Folk Art Heart
Half A—R & L

Folk Art Heart
¾" Circle

Folk Art Heart
A

Folk Art Heart
B

Folk Art Heart
Cowboy

Folk Art Heart
C

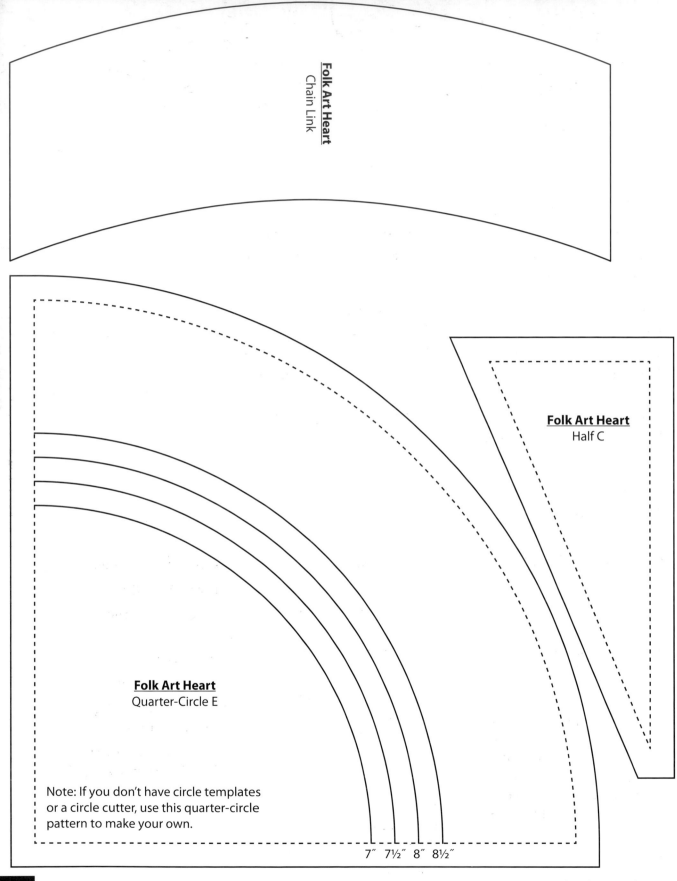

Folk Art Heart
Chain Link

Folk Art Heart
Half C

Folk Art Heart
Quarter-Circle E

Note: If you don't have circle templates
or a circle cutter, use this quarter-circle
pattern to make your own.

7″ 7½″ 8″ 8½″

over grown

This quilt was inspired by my Celebrate fabric collection for FreeSpirit Fabrics. It is an exercise in using a collection of warm and cool colors to add impact to a design. The cool colors (blues, greens, and purples) move vertically and the warm colors (reds, yellows, and oranges) move horizontally.

The appliqué pieces are set off using dark or brown fabrics. Often I hear people complaining about brown as an "ugly" color, but in truth it is a beautiful neutral that allows colors to shine as they would in a real garden. The dark gives strength to the lines. It is also interesting to note that the outer borders and some of the strips are made with Kaffe Fassett's Artisan Stripe. The fabric looks like it is pieced, but it isn't! Don't be afraid to use a lot of print fabrics here for exciting results!

TECHNIQUES

Needle-turn appliqué

Organic bias stems

MATERIALS

Yardage is based on 42″ width of fabric unless otherwise noted.

CENTER RECTANGLE AND APPLIQUÉ: ⅓ yard (30 cm) of floral print

INNER BORDERS:

- **VERTICAL:**

  COOL PRINTS: ⅛ yard (15 cm) *each* of 3 different prints and ⅓ yard (35 cm) *each* of 4 different prints

- **HORIZONTAL:**

  WARM PRINTS: ⅛ yard (15 cm) *each* of 2 different prints and ⅓ yard (35 cm) *each* of 4 different prints (If you wish to cut longer borders on lengthwise grain to avoid piecing, you will need 1⅓ yards of 1 warm print.)

APPLIQUÉ BORDER:

- **PINK SPOT:** 1⅓ yards (1.2 m)

- **GREEN SPOT:** 1⅞ yards (1.7 m)

- **STEMS:** ⅝ yard (60 cm)

- **FLOWERS AND LEAVES:** Fat quarters of an assortment of fabrics, including a variety of dark, medium, and cool colors

OUTER BORDERS:

The warm/cool relationship has been established. For the outer rings the fabrics simply frame the quilt.

- **CORNERS:**

  ROUND 1 (BROWN CIRCLES): ⅞ yard (85 cm)

  ROUND 2 (SPOTTED FLORAL): 1⅛ yards (1 m)

  ROUND 3 (BLUE STRIPES): 1⅛ yards (1 m)

- **CENTERS:**

  GREEN SPOT: ⅜ yard (35 cm)

  PINK SPOT: ½ yard (50 cm)

BACKING: 8⅛ yards (7.5 m)

BATTING: 96″ × 96″ (245 cm × 245 cm)

BINDING: ¾ yard (75 cm)

APPLIQUÉ SUPPLIES, including Wash-Away Appliqué Sheets

QUILTING THREADS: 3 different spools of Eleganza variegated perle cotton #8

Making the Quilt

The cutting for this quilt is done in conjunction with the piecing.

NOTE

It doesn't matter if your strips are the exact same size as the ones in the pattern, only that your quilt is square. Be sure to measure through the middle of each step from top to bottom or side to side and adjust your strips as you progress. Make any needed alterations to the size of your strip.

INNER BORDERS

Refer to the inner border assembly diagram (page 104).

STEP 1

CENTER: Cut 1 rectangle 4½″ × 8½″. It is possible to use a different-size center. Simply adjust further strips in the process if you would like a bigger feature print here.

STEP 2

Cut 2 cool strips 1½″ × 8½″.

Match the middle of the center rectangle to the middle of the strip, and pin the ends to match. Sew in place. Repeat this process for each round. This is critical for keeping the quilt square as it grows.

STEP 3

Cut 2 warm strips 2″ × 6½″.

Join to the top and bottom of Step 1.

STEP 4

Cut 2 cool strips 2½″ × 11½″.

Join to the sides of Step 2.

STEP 5

Cut 2 warm strips 3″ × 10½″.

Join to the top and bottom of Step 3.

STEP 6

Cut 2 cool strips 2″ × 16½″.

Join to the sides of Step 4.

STEP 7

Cut 2 warm strips 2½″ × 13½″.

Join to the top and bottom of Step 5.

STEP 8

Cut 2 cool strips 3½″ × 20½″.

Join to the sides of Step 6.

STEP 9

Cut 2 warm strips 2″ × 19½″.

Join to the top and bottom of Step 7.

STEP 10

Cut 2 cool strips 4″ × 23½″.

Join to the sides of Step 8.

STEP 11

Cut 2 warm strips 3½″ × 26½″.

Join to the top and bottom of Step 9.

STEP 12

Cut 2 cool strips 4½″ × 29½″.

Join to the sides of Step 10.

STEP 13

Cut 2 warm strips 3½″ × 34½″.

Join to the top and bottom of Step 11.

STEP 14

Cut 2 cool strips 4″ × 35½″.

Join to the sides of Step 12.

STEP 15

Cut 2 warm strips 3″ × 41½″

Join to the top and bottom of Step 13.

STEP 16

Cut 2 cool strips 3″ × 40½″.

Join to the sides of Step 14.

STEP 17

Cut 3 warm strips 3½″ × width of fabric. Sew together end to end and subcut into 2 strips 3½″ × 46½″. (If you have enough fabric, just cut the 2 strips 3½″ × 46½″ from the lengthwise grain.)

Join to the top and bottom of Step 15.

APPLIQUÉ BORDER

1. Cut 2 warm strips 10½″ × 46½″ for the top and bottom borders.

2. Cut 2 cool strips 10½″ × 66½″ for the side borders.

3. See Appliqué (below) to prepare and appliqué the shapes onto these strips.

4. Join the warm appliqué borders to the top and bottom of the quilt. Join the longer cool borders to the sides.

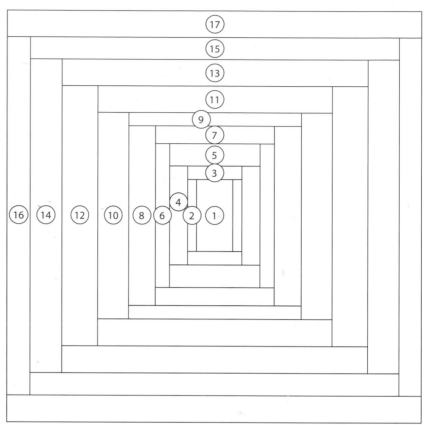

Inner border assembly

Appliqué

The appliqué is done using wash-away appliqué paper and the bias-stem, needle-turn appliqué, and fussy-cut viewing template methods from the Chapter 2: Making It Happen (page 33). No matter what you do, have fun with it!

Varying the size, position, and placement of the flowers will add your personal hand to the project. I used the following, layering shapes for added interest, but feel free to add any size or shape of flowers you might like to personalize your project:

- 24 leaves in a variety of sizes

- 4 paisley flowers

- 6 large flowers

- 3 medium flowers (the lower portion of the large flower)

- 6 small flowers

- Bias stems: 4 longer bias stems with thicker bases, from 28″ to 22″ long; 4 medium stems; and 12 short thin stems, anywhere from 3″ to 10″

NOTE

Keep in mind that you do not need to recreate the exact placement of the stems in the quilt. Build your stems organically. The bases of the stems are about 3½″ finished and the narrow ends are about ½″. The shape should flow from wide to narrow. Generally, I make a lot of stems at the same time, with most of the stem being more narrow so that bits can be cut for offshoots.

Appliqué Placement

1. Fold the appliqué background in half and finger-press the fold. Lay it out flat and position the shapes so that the stems grow out from the middle and extend to the edges of the strips.

2. Position the smaller stems behind the longer, bigger stems, as they will need to be secured first. Use light dabs of the appliqué glue to dot a line and then position the stems over the glue line. Finger-press in place.

3. Appliqué the layers of the flowers and leaves before positioning them on the background.

4. Pin or baste the flowers and leaves; appliqué in place.

OUTER BORDERS

Follow the same method as for the inner borders to cut and attach 1 set of pieced borders at a time to ensure a square quilt top, but now the top and bottom strips will be added before the side strips.

TOP AND BOTTOM ROUND 1:

Cut 4 strips 3½″ × 31½″ from the brown circles fabric.

Cut 2 strips 3½″ × 4½″ from the green spot fabric for the center piece.

Join a long strip to each side of a center piece; make 2.

Join to the top and bottom appliqué borders.

SIDES ROUND 1:

Cut 4 strips 3½″ × 31″ from the brown circles fabric.

Cut 2 strips 3½″ × 11½″ from the pink spot fabric for the center.

Join a long strip to each side of a center piece; make 2.

Join to the side appliqué borders.

TOP AND BOTTOM ROUND 2:

Cut 4 strips 4½″ × 31″ from the spotted floral fabric.

Cut 2 strips 4½″ × 11½″ from the green spot fabric for the center.

Join a long rectangle to each side of a center piece; make 2.

Join to the top and bottom brown circles borders.

SIDES ROUND 2:

Cut 4 strips 4½″ × 30½″ from the spotted floral fabric.

Cut 2 strips 4½″ × 20½″ from the pink spot fabric for the center.

Join a long rectangle to each side of a center piece; make 2.

Join to the side brown circles borders.

TOP AND BOTTOM ROUND 3:

Cut 4 strips 4½″ × 30½″ from the blue stripes.

Cut 2 strips 4½″ × 20½″ from the green spot fabric for the center.

Join a long rectangle to each side of a center piece; make 2.

Join to the top and bottom spotted floral borders.

SIDES ROUND 3:

Cut 4 strips 4½″ × 30″ from the blue stripes.

Cut 2 strips 4½″ × 29½″ from the pink spot fabric for the center.

Join a long rectangle to each side of a center piece; make 2.

Join to the side spotted floral borders.

Quilting

Over Grown was quilted using three colors of variegated perle cotton #8. The quilt lines follow the rounds of the piecing in irregularly spaced lines. It is important when quilting to cover the quilt equally until the outside of the quilt. It is tempting to space the lines further apart as you near the border, but doing this may cause the quilt to "wrinkle" in the borders. Consistent coverage helps to keep a quilt square.

Quilt assembly

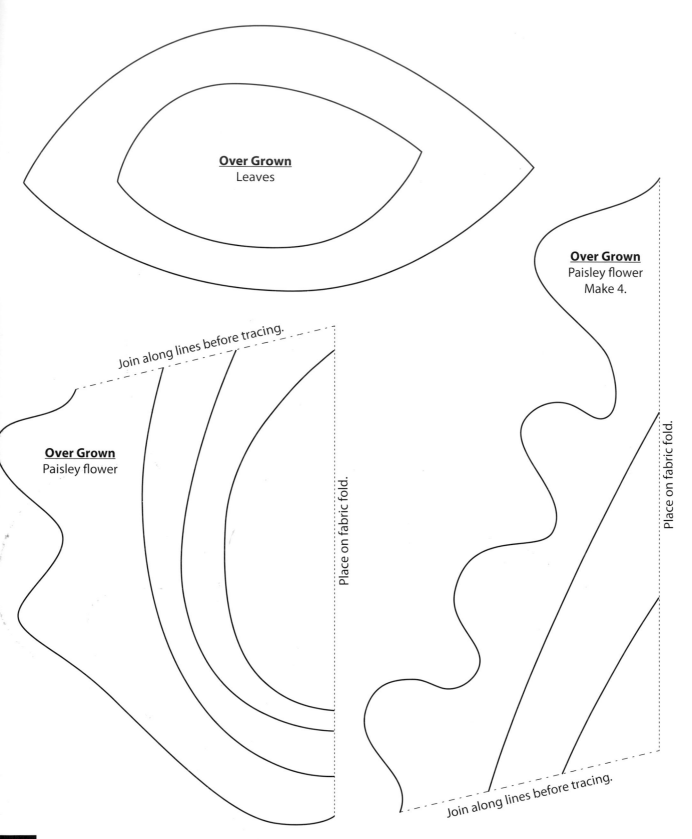

Over Grown
Leaves

Over Grown
Paisley flower
Make 4.

Over Grown
Paisley flower

Join along lines before tracing.

Place on fabric fold.

Place on fabric fold.

Join along lines before tracing.

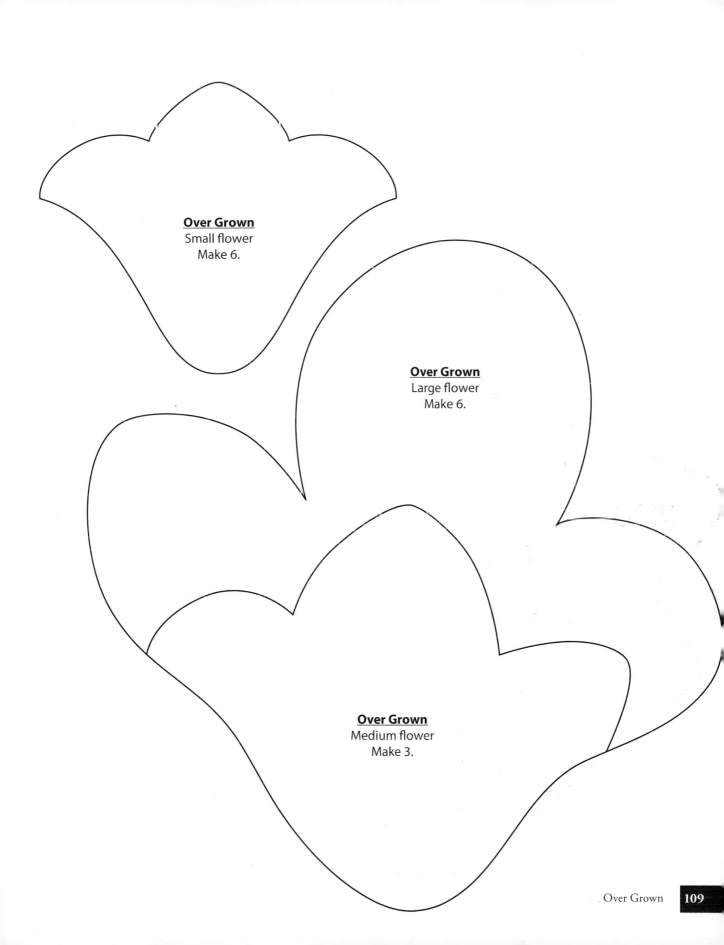

Over Grown
Small flower
Make 6.

Over Grown
Large flower
Make 6.

Over Grown
Medium flower
Make 3.

TECHNIQUES

Needle-turn appliqué

Organic bias vines

Freestyle flower arranging!

A weekend appeared on my horizon with two free days. I was captivated by the idea of just doing something spontaneous, so I hacked into my stash, using whatever my hands fell upon. I turned the radio up loud; grabbed some idle sketches; and made a pile of shot-cotton plaids, checks, and stripes for backgrounds. They have an airy lightness to them that reminded me of that smell of spring in the air. Of course, the middle block is the highlight color to keep the quilt balanced.

To capture large-scale prints in one shape, I made a simple vase. For the flowers, I went a bit mad and just did whatever came to my head. They are all easy to recreate as shapes or can be altered to capture flower shapes found in existing textiles. Look for prints that have a motifs that might translate into flowers. Maybe literally, but maybe not! Curves, paisley prints, spots … let your imagination run wild.

The sashing and the border are purposefully black and white. A variety of prints and colors can be tied together quite easily using black-and-white prints. I love a good check, and the placement in the sashing strips not only unifies the blocks but gives it a happy picnic kind of feeling. The border print by Alexander Henry has bunnies hopping around, which appealed to the springlike qualities of the quilt.

Repeat it as you see it, but listen to your heart, consider your personal stash, and go with the flow. If you find flowers with different shapes, go for it!

MATERIALS

Yardage is based on 42˝ width of fabric unless otherwise noted.

PLAIDS, CHECKS, AND STRIPES: ½–⅝ yard (50–60 cm) *each* of 9 different fabrics, depending on how you choose to orient the pattern (you will need a 15˝ × 21˝ rectangle from each) for block backgrounds

BLACK/WHITE CHECK: 1 yard (0.9 m) for sashing

NOTE

If you want to use fat quarters for the backgrounds, check the size and be aware that you will have to position the fat quarter sideways, with the long sides running vertically. Be sure the pattern works before you choose a fat quarter.

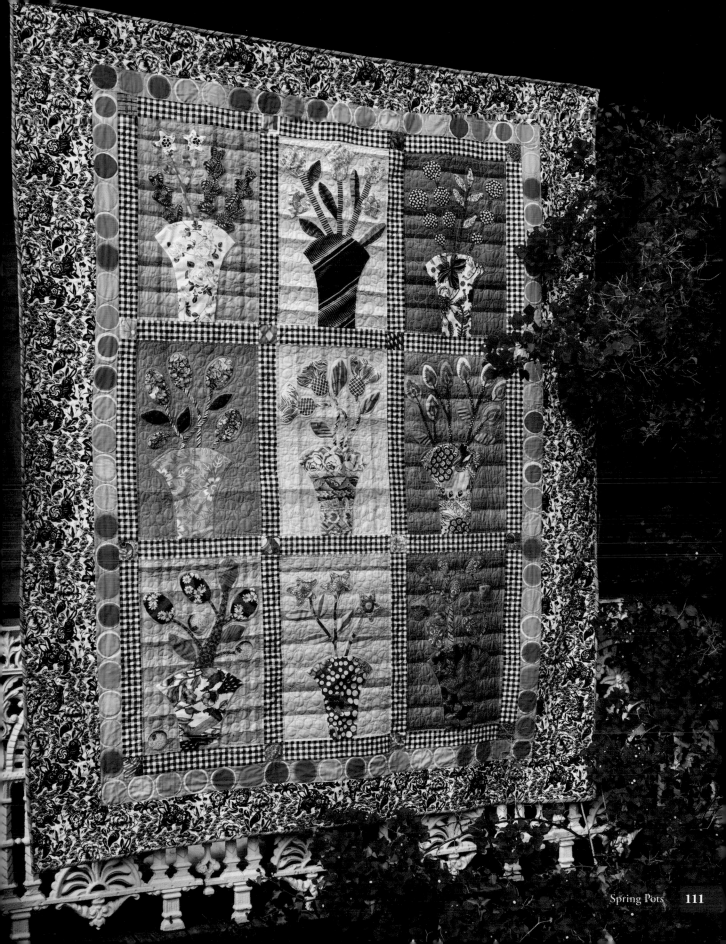

ASSORTED PRINTS:

- 9 fat quarters for pots

- 9–15 fat quarters or scraps for flowers

- 9 fat quarters for stems

- 9 fat quarters for leaves

INNER BORDER: ¾ yard (70 cm; more if fussy cutting)

OUTER BORDER: 2¼ yards (2.1 m)

BACKING: 5⅜ yards (5 m)

BATTING: 85″ × 94″ (220 cm × 240 cm)

BINDING: ¾ yard (70 cm)

APPLIQUÉ SUPPLIES, including Wash-Away Appliqué Sheets

VARIEGATED MACHINE QUILTING THREAD

CUTTING

Plaids, checks, and stripes

- Cut 9 backgrounds 15″ × 21″. These are oversized; you will trim them to 14½ × 20½″ after appliqué.

Black/white check

- Cut 12 strips 2½″ × 14½″ for the horizontal sashing strips.

- Cut 12 strips 2½″ × 20½″ for the vertical sashing strips.

Assorted prints

- Cut 16 squares 2½″ × 2½″ for the cornerstones.

- Cut 9 vases from a variety of your favorite fabrics using light, medium, and dark fabrics.

- Use the patterns (pages 115 and 116) or create your own shapes for 9 different kinds of flowers, leaves, and stems. Note that some stems are cut straight and some are cut using the bias method (page 36).

Inner border

- Cut 6 strips 3½″ × width of fabric (7 strips if the width of fabric is only 42″ or less). Join end to end and subcut:

  2 strips 3½″ × 68½″ for the side borders

  2 strips 3½″ × 56½″ for the top and bottom borders

Outer border

- Cut 4 strips 11″ × width of fabric. Join end to end and subcut:

  2 strips 11″ × 74½″ for the side borders

- Cut 4 strips 6½″ × width of fabric. Join end to end and subcut:

  2 strips 6½″ × 77½″ for the top and bottom borders

Making the Quilt

APPLIQUÉ BLOCKS

Refer to Needle-Turn Appliqué (page 34) for instructions on preparing appliqué shapes, basting, and stitching.

1. Position the prepared appliqué shapes and pin or baste before sewing them in place. Be free with the design placement. It isn't critical to have them exactly as pictured. Start with the vase and then the stems before adding the flowers. If there are shapes with layers, appliqué the shapes first.

2. Trim each of the 9 appliqué blocks to 14½″ × 20½″.

ASSEMBLY

1. Position the 9 blocks on the design wall. Keep in mind that the darkest block will rest most comfortably in the bottom right-hand corner. The lightest block in my quilt is in the middle for balance.

2. Lay out the sashing strips and cornerstones.

3. Join the sashing strips and corner squares in horizontal rows.

4. Join the blocks with sashing strips.

5. Sew the rows together.

6. Measure the quilt through the middle for the true width and length. Adjust borders where necessary to reflect your measurements.

7. Join the side inner borders and then the inner top and bottom borders.

8. Repeat for the outer border.

Quilt assembly

Quilting

I wanted to fill the backgrounds with quilting while allowing the appliqué to pop out. For each of the different areas, I used a different fill pattern.

The blocks have a freestyle bubble fill and an echo line around the appliqué shapes. The sashing strips have a meandering vine that moves along the length of each strip. The circle print is outlined in curved lines. The outer border uses a fan shape that I noted in the border print. In all cases, the lines are fairly organic and relaxed, as this is a fun-feeling project.

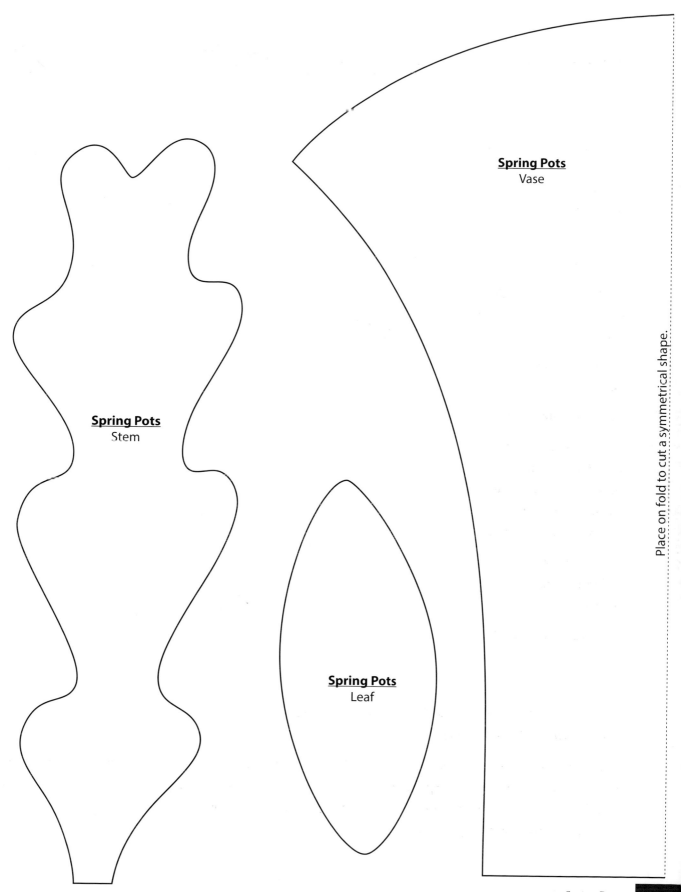

Spring Pots
Vase

Spring Pots
Stem

Spring Pots
Leaf

Place on fold to cut a symmetrical shape.

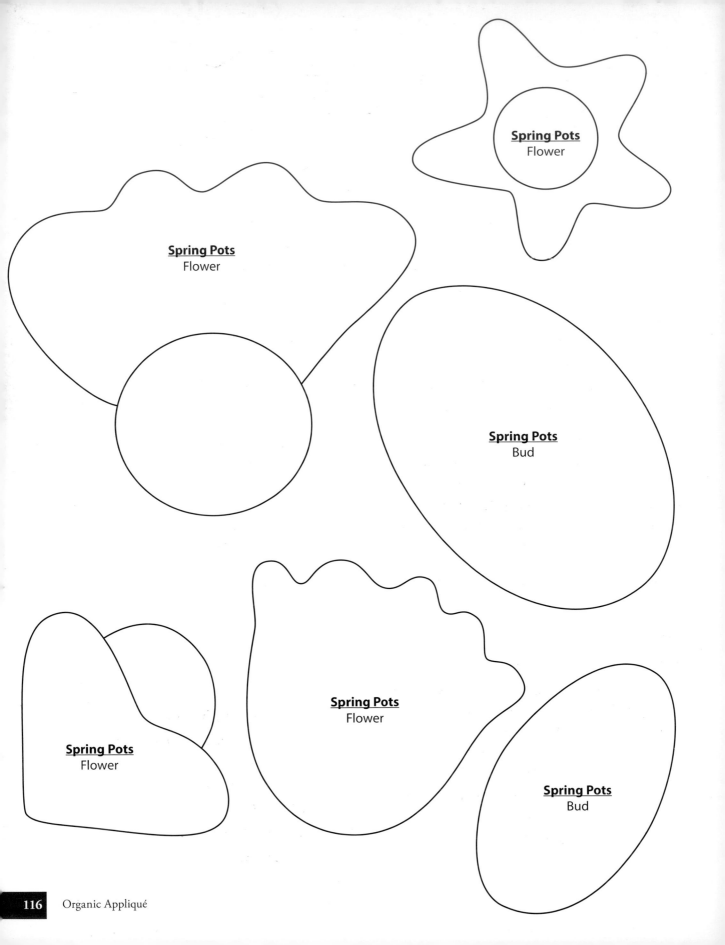

Spring Pots
Flower

Spring Pots
Flower

Spring Pots
Bud

Spring Pots
Flower

Spring Pots
Flower

Spring Pots
Bud

organic churn dash

I am surrounded by talented designers all the time. Over the years, I have picked up several wonderful techniques to practice in my quilts. This is a great use of the bias-stem method that I learned from Sue Cody many years ago. I love how organic and unique it is to every project.

Additionally, I have practiced looking at fabric and wondering what it can do for a long time. Using fabric effectively is a great way to make the quilts look a bit more complicated than they actually are! Here, in my flowers, I have captured a different perspective on a Kaffe Fassett print. When he saw it, he got very excited that I didn't use it as he had intended! Score!

Let the twists and turns of the stems make your quilt into something unique to you! It is critical to make this quilt on the design wall so that the lines of the blocks can connect. I also concentrated on having a nice mix of warm and cool prints for the Churn Dash blocks. The backgrounds work as the same, but there are three different prints that react equally. I find that reproduction prints are great for stems, but in this case I used the Chain Link Check from my Horizons collection.

Find a border that brings the blocks to life!

TECHNIQUES

Needle-turn appliqué

Bias vines

Piecing

MATERIALS

Yardage is based on 42″ width of fabric unless otherwise noted.

LIGHT PRINTS: ½ yard (50 cm) each of 2 different prints for Churn Dash block backgrounds and ¾ yard (70 cm) for appliquéd border background

ASSORTED BRIGHT PRINTS: Scraps up to ¼ yard (25 cm) *each* of 14–19 fabrics for blocks

SMALL BLACK-AND-WHITE SPOT PRINT: 1 yard (90 cm) for alternating rectangles in blocks

OUTER BORDER: 1½ yards (1.4 m)

APPLIQUÉ FABRICS:

• **DARK PLAID:** ⅝ yard (½ m) for stems

• **FLORAL PRINTS:** ⅓ yard (30 cm) *each* of 3 prints for fussy cutting flowers

• **LEAFY PRINT:** ⅓ yard (30 cm)

BACKING: 4⅞ yards (4.5 m)

BATTING: 72″ × 84″ (185 cm × 215 cm)

BINDING: ⅝ yard (65 cm)

APPLIQUÉ SUPPLIES

CUTTING

Light prints

From each of the first 2 background prints:

- Cut 2 strips 8½" × width of fabric. Subcut:

  6 squares 8½" × 8½" from each strip (12 total)

From the third light print:

- Cut 3 strips 8½" × width of fabric. Join 2 of the strips end to end and subcut a strip 8½" × 56½" for the side strip appliqué.

  From the remaining strip, subcut a strip 8½" × 36½" for the bottom appliqué.

Assorted bright prints

NOTE: *A traditional Churn Dash block would require 4 rectangles 2½" × 8½" and 2 squares 4⅞" × 4⅞". This quilt has 6 complete blocks and several partial and deconstructed blocks. Mix and match as you like using your favorite fabrics, or follow my cutting instructions below.*

From each of 6 fabrics:

- Cut 1 strip 5" × width of fabric and subcut:

  2 squares 5" × 5". Trim to 4⅞" × 4⅞".

  4 rectangles 2½" × 8½"

From each of 5 fabrics:

- Cut 1 square 4⅞" × 4⅞".

- Cut 1 rectangle 2½" × 8½".

From each of 4 fabrics:

- Cut 1 rectangle 2½" × 8½".

From each of 3 fabrics:

- Cut 2 squares 4⅞" × 4⅞".

- Cut 2 rectangles 2½" × 8½".

From 1 fabric:

- Cut 2 squares 4⅞" × 4⅞" and 3 rectangles 2½" × 8½".

Crosscut all the 4⅞" squares in half diagonally.

Small black-and-white spot print:

- Cut 11 strips 2½" × width of fabric. Subcut 41 rectangles 2½" × 8½".

- Cut 1 strip 4⅞" × width of fabric. Subcut 5 squares; cut each in half on the diagonal.

Outer border

- Cut 4 strips 4½" × width of fabric and join end to end in pairs. Subcut:

  1 strip 4½" × 60½" (top)   1 strip 4½" × 76½" (left side)

- Cut 3 strips 8½" × width of fabric (4 strips if width of fabric is less than 42"). Join the strips end to end and subcut:

  1 strip 8½" × 60½" (bottom)   1 strip 8½" × 64½" (right side)

Making the Quilt

APPLIQUÉ

Refer to Needle-Turn Appliqué (page 34) for instructions on preparing appliqué shapes, basting, and stitching.

1. Use the appliqué patterns (pages 122 and 124) or create your own flowers based on your fabrics. It's helpful to make a viewing template (using what remains after cutting away the shape from a sheet of wash-away appliqué paper) for the different shapes and to explore the fabric options to maximize the impact of each fabric in the shapes.

The fabric that I used for most of the flowers is Sunburst by Kaffe Fassett for Westminster. It has a pansy centered in stripes. The tendency is to use the fabric in strips with the pansy centered, but in this case I used the space between the flowers to define my shapes.

The sample has the following elements:

- **3 LARGE BELL FLOWERS**

- **7 MEDIUM WAVY FLOWERS**

- **3 FUNKY FLOWERS**

- **12 ROUND FLOWER BUDS OF VARIED SIZES:** Use the circles from *Stolen Moments* (page 69).

- **31 LEAVES OF VARIOUS SIZES:** For varied leaf sizes, use the inside portions of the wash-away appliqué paper from the bigger leaves, or see *Stolen Moments* (page 69) for more leaf patterns.

Tip Achieving variation in the sizes of the leaves is easy. Start big with cutting leaves from the wash-away appliqué paper and use the inner pieces to make smaller shapes. You can also make variations of the flower shapes provided, as I did. Draw in an extra petal to the funky flowers or smooth out the curves on a shape—it's up to you.

2. Prepare about 4½ yards (4 m) of bias stems (page 36), separated into sections 1—1½ yards long and ½″–3″ wide. You may need a few extra-thin stems as well.

CHURN DASH BLOCKS

1. Referring to the quilt assembly diagram (next page), arrange the bright-print Churn Dash rectangles and half-square triangles on the design wall. Alternate the warm and cool colors across the quilt.

2. Add the black-and-white spot alternate rectangles and half-square triangles around the blocks.

3. Add the 2 light appliqué border strips and the remaining Churn Dash / alternate sets to the bottom and right side so you can see the complete flow of colors across the quilt top.

NOTE

Keep in mind that the heavy or darker colors will rest comfortably in the bottom right corner. I chose some warm and some cool colors and alternated them throughout the quilt. Note that the top right-hand corner is only a partial block, so in that case I used one of my darker fabrics to stabilize the other dark block in the opposite corner.

4. Position the 8½″ background squares between the Churn Dash rectangles, alternating the fabrics used.

5. Arrange the appliqué elements on the block backgrounds so that the stems weave throughout the blocks. Review the placement of colors in the Churn Dash shapes. When you're happy with all the appliqué positions, make note of the block placement and then stitch the appliqué down to the block backgrounds and inner border strips.

ASSEMBLY

1. Reposition the appliquéd block backgrounds and borders on the design wall.

2. Join the Churn Dash rectangles and alternate rectangles; then join the half-square triangles. Reposition on the wall.

3. Join the horizontal Churn Dash / alternate rectangle sets and half-square triangles in rows.

4. Join the appliquéd block backgrounds and the Churn Dash / alternate rectangle sets in rows.

5. Join the rows together to complete the 12-block section.

6. Add the Churn Dash / alternate rectangle set to the left side of the bottom appliqué border and join to the quilt.

7. Join the pieced rectangles to the top of the side appliqué border and sew it to the right side of the quilt.

8. Sew the Churn Dash / alternate rectangles and half-square triangles together for the bottom row and join it to the quilt. Do the same with the pieced rectangles and half-square triangles in the right column.

Quilt assembly

OUTER BORDER

1. Join an 8½″ × 64½″ border strip to the right side of the quilt.

2. Add the 8½″ × 60½″ border to the bottom.

3. Sew the 4½″ × 60½″ border to the top.

4. Sew the 4½″ × 76½″ border to the left side of the quilt.

Organic Churn Dash
Large leaf

Organic Churn Dash
Small leaf

Quilting

Organic Churn Dash is hand quilted with perle cotton #8. The lines are around the appliqué, which makes it stand out ever so slightly. Then the Churn Dash blocks have quilting lines just inside the seam allowance. On the outer borders, I ran two to three squiggle lines to curve through the leaves. There isn't a lot of quilting on this quilt, which I think makes it soft and cuddly.

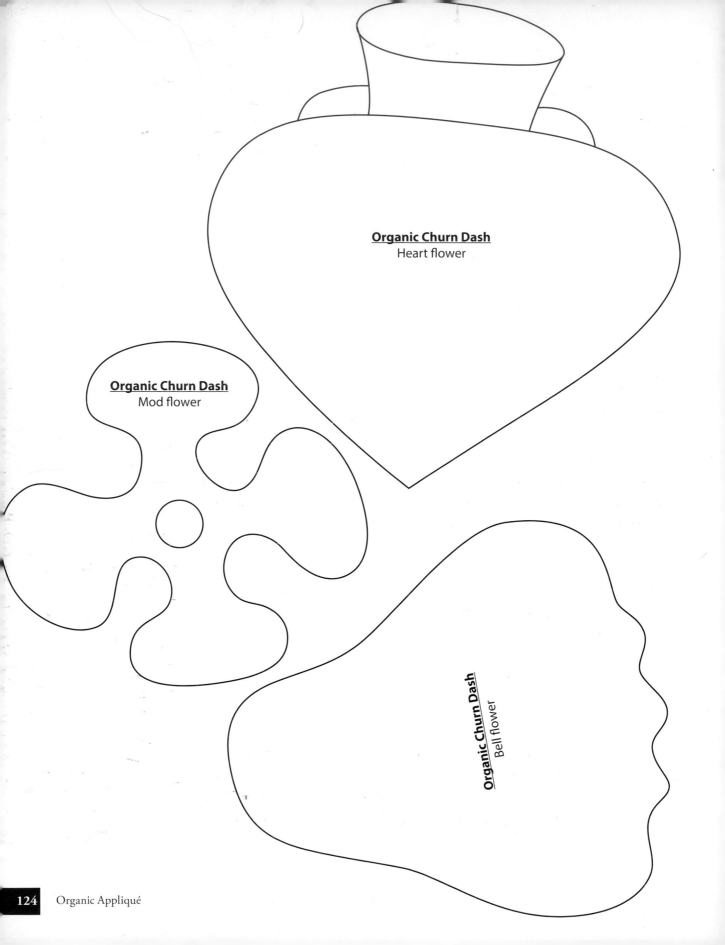

Organic Churn Dash
Heart flower

Organic Churn Dash
Mod flower

Organic Churn Dash
Bell flower

boro collage

FINISHED QUILT: 41½″ × 47½″ (105 cm × 121 cm)

NOTE

Your finished size will be dependent on the size of the fabrics used

Boro appliqué comes from the Japanese practice of mending. Old clothes are covered with patches placed over worn-out areas and simply stitched in place with repetitive lines of stitching. The result is an engaging textile that begs to be touched for the texture and memories obviously sewn into each piece. Think sashiko- or kantha-style stitching for this one, and if you are unfamiliar, a quick internet search of boro stitching will give you a huge variety of ideas.

The little vase was a practice piece using circles, and I enjoy the way it mirrors the larger vase composition both in color and shapes.

Working with different textured fabrics can open doors to interesting designs. In this quilt I have used a variety of different-weight fabrics, including wovens and linens mixed with regular quilting cottons. The mix creates a collage of ideas that work together to create a unique composition. The thing is I have collected these bits and pieces over many years and have had them stored away for someday. It was with great pleasure that I started pulling out the Japanese fabrics and actually used them in a quilt.

TECHNIQUES

Boro stitching

Needle-turn appliqué

Bias stems

Composition

Look for bits of unfinished projects that might find a home here.

MATERIALS

NOTE: *If you are working with fabrics that you already have in your stash, your yardage requirements will be based on the sizes of your particular pieces and how you arrange them. Use this list as a general guide.*

Yardage is based on 42″ width of fabric unless otherwise noted.

BACKGROUND FABRICS:

- **MAIN:** 1 yard (1 m; yellow stripe)

- **SIDE PANEL:** ½ yard or 1⅛ yards (.5 m or 1 m, depending on the orientation of the print; my floral piece measured 14½″ × 34″.)

- **BOTTOM PANEL:** 1¼ yards (1.2 m; I used a rectangle 14½″ × 42″ of a striped brown fabric.)

- **PIECED SIDE BORDER:** ⅜ yard (35 cm) *each* of 2 fabrics (I used a pink ikat and a black-and-purple stripe.)

APPLIQUÉ FABRICS:

- **TRIANGLE STRIP:** ⅓ yard (35 cm; aqua stripe)

- **LARGE VASE:** 1 fat quarter (woven stripe)

- **LARGE LEAVES:** 1 fat quarter (woven dot)

- **STEM:** 1 fat quarter

- **SMALL VASE ARRANGEMENT:** 3–6 assorted fat quarters or scraps

- **MISCELLANEOUS FLORAL SCRAPS** for boro appliqué

BACKING: 3 yards (3 m)

BATTING: 49″ × 55″ (125 cm × 140 cm)

BINDING: ½ yard (50 cm)

RIBBON: 1 yard (1 m) of your choice

APPLIQUÉ SUPPLIES

VARIEGATED QUILTING THREADS: 3 spools of Eleganza variegated perle cotton #8

SASHIKO NEEDLES *or* **CLOVER EMBROIDERY NEEDLES, PACKET SIZE 3–9**

60° (EQUILATERAL) TRIANGLE TEMPLATE, at least 8″ high, for marking appliqué

ISOSCELES TRIANGLE TEMPLATE *or* **WEDGE RULER,** in your desired angle, to cut side border (I used a 67.5°/45° triangle.)

CUTTING

The backgrounds for this piece are what they are because of the shapes of the fabrics that I wanted to use. There is an appeal to quilts made using what is available that is sometimes hard to achieve when planned. Consider making a grouping of what you have on hand that is pleasing to the eye and using the shapes they suggest. Cut as you sew and appliqué sections. Here is what mine were:

Main background

- Cut 1 rectangle 20″ × 34″.

Triangle appliqué

- Cut 1 rectangle 10″ × 34″ (or to fit the length of your main background piece).

Side panel

- Cut 1 rectangle 14½″ × 34″ (or to fit the length of your main background piece).

Bottom panel background

- Cut 1 rectangle 14½″ × 36″ (or to fit the width of your assembled upper piece).

Pieced side border

From each of the 2 fabrics:

- Cut 1 strip 6½″ × width of fabric.

Appliqué

- See Making the Quilt (below) to cut the pieces as you work on the quilt.

Making the Quilt

MAIN PANEL

1. First, prepare the vertical appliquéd triangle strip (the 10″-wide aqua piece in my quilt). Use a 60° triangle template and a chalk pencil (I like the thick crayon one from Bohin). Starting in the middle of the strip, trace the 60° triangle shape to your desired height—mine are about 8″. Work from the center outward to balance the triangles equally along the length. This chalk line is the sewing line.

2. Pin (or baste by hand or machine) the marked strip to the left side of the main background piece, using the chalk outlines of the triangles to center the strip. When you are happy with your placement, add a pen line ¼″ outside the chalk lines of the triangles. This line will be your cutting line.

3. Pin inside the chalk line and cut a section of the pen line to release the bulk. Use your fingers to fold back and press the cut edge.

4. Start stitching at one end and needle-turn appliqué the edges of the triangles to the background piece. Refer to the directions for appliquéing inner and outer points (page 40) to help you secure each.

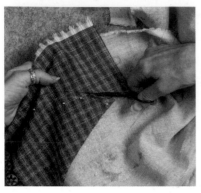 

Note: My demonstration fabrics differ from the appliquéd triangle strip in the quilt.

Tip Cutting small sections at a time keeps the bias edges from fraying as you stitch.

5. Pin and sew a length of decorative ribbon on top of the appliquéd triangle strip. Prepare 4 fussy-cut circles and space them evenly along the ribbon; then appliqué them in place.

Large Pot of Flowers

1. Prepare 4 bias stems approximately 8″–12″ long and varying in width from 2″ to ½″.

2. Use Wash-Away Appliqué Sheets (page 34) to prepare the large vase and several leaves, basting the edges under before you place them on the background. Use perle cotton #8 to appliqué these pieces with a running stitch right along the turned edge. The turned edges will be a nice contrast to the boro appliqué.

3. For the boro appliqué, cut the flowers with a bit of excess around each motif. I layered a circular flower print on top of larger irregular florals and used a smaller section of the same floral for a bud. Place them over the bias stem ends. Stitch in place using perle cotton #8 and repetitive lines of stitching that cover the piece and extend past the raw edges. It is a good idea to leave a bit of space between the rows of stitching so that later you can add quilting stitches between the appliqué stitches.

If you like, save some flower motifs to add to the bottom left corner of the assembled quilt top.

Small Pot of Flowers

Make this little pot of circle flowers on a background rectangle; then add it to the bottom panel. If you have an already completed appliqué piece that would work well here, consider appliquéing it to the bottom panel instead of starting a new piece.

1. Use Wash-Away Appliqué Sheets to prepare the following shapes and baste the edges under. Arrange on a 8½″ × 12½″ background rectangle and needle-turn appliqué the shapes in place.

- 1 rectangle 4½″ × 8½″ for the table

- 5 decorative strips approximately 1½″ × 4½″ (here, 3 plaid and 2 print)

- 1 pot with handle

- 6 leaves

- 4 circles 1½″

- 5 circles 2″

2. Join the appliquéd background rectangle to the bottom panel using an appliqué stitch or boro if you prefer.

Mini vase collage

TRIANGLE SIDE BORDER

1. Place the 2 fabric strips 6½″ wide right sides together. Use an isosceles triangle template or a wedge ruler to subcut very blunt-tipped triangles (that is, wedges) from each fabric, rotating the template with each cut. I used 4 pink and 5 black and purple. The number needed will depend on the proportions of your ruler and how it is placed.

Mine were cut by aligning the base of the 9″ high template with the top point extending beyond the edge of the fabric, making a fat wedge shape. You

may choose to do it this way or use a more conventional method of making a border of triangles.

2. Join the blunt-tip triangles in a row, alternating the colors and orientation. Make your triangle strip long enough to fit along the right side of the quilt when assembled. You will trim it to fit later.

ASSEMBLY

When the vases are appliquéd, join the backgrounds to make the top.

1. Join the side panel to the panel with the large vase of flowers.

2. Join the bottom panel to the quilt.

3. Measure the assembled quilt top vertically through the center. Trim the end triangles of the side border as needed to fit. Sew to the right side of the quilt top.

4. Use boro stitching to add some more scrappy squares, rectangles, and flowers to the lower left corner, including some that go over the seamlines. Keep adding until you love the way it looks!

Quilt assembly

QUILTING

The quilting on *Boro Collage* is very organic. I had already done a lot of stitching on the piece and needed to blend the quilting with the boro stitching. I used a color that matched the background for most of the quilting and stitched between the boro lines where necessary. In other areas, the stitching follows the lines of the fabrics used for the different sections. For example, quilting lines go through the stripes at the base and around the appliquéd arrangement in the bottom panel.

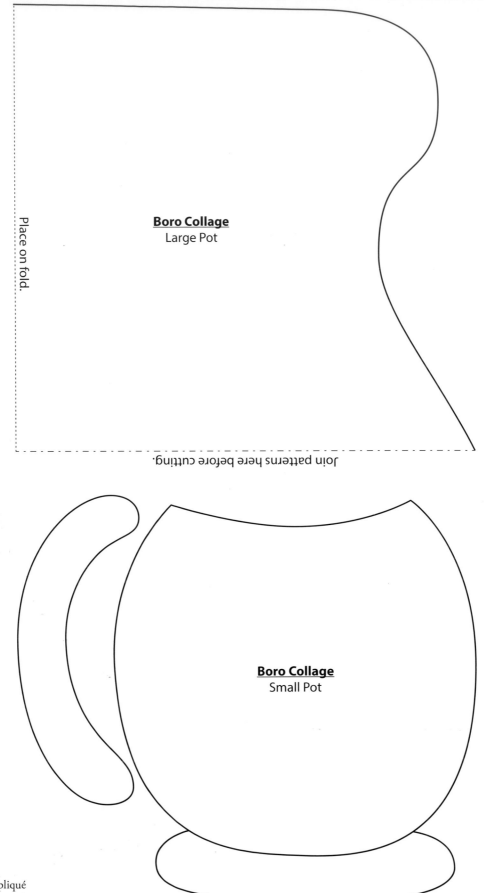

Place on fold.

Boro Collage
Large Pot

Join patterns here before cutting.

Boro Collage
Small Pot

Join patterns here before cutting.

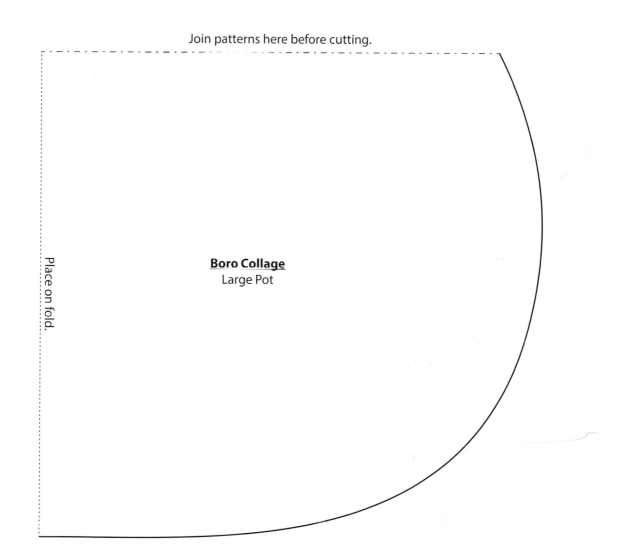

Boro Collage
Large Pot

Place on fold.

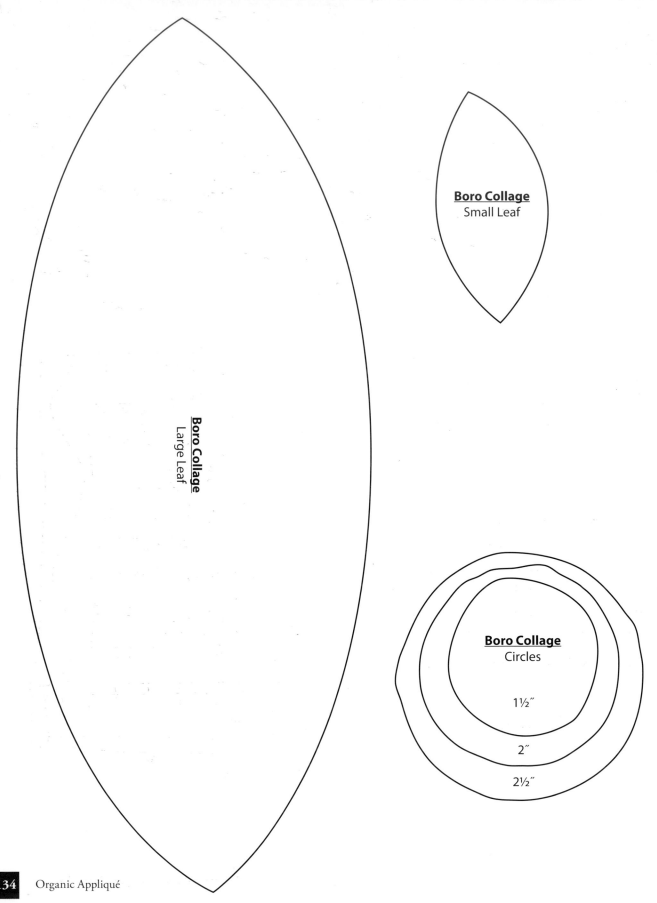

Boro Collage
Small Leaf

Boro Collage
Large Leaf

Boro Collage
Circles

1½"

2"

2½"

black bird fly: a design exercise

FINISHED QUILT: 43″ × 56″ (110 cm × 143 cm)

Black Bird Fly is a very free-form, organic style of construction. The quilt started as a sketch of a flower. I am including it to give you a starting point or springboard for composing a unique project of your own.

The Design Process

STEP 1: START WITH A SKETCH

The idea started as a sketch. I drew an imaginary flower shape on paper. I had a bit of an idea about how to draw it, but mostly I just want to record an idea. Your ideas could come from a photo, a painting, or an image online. Here are a couple of considerations:

• Draw smooth, flowing lines that are easy to appliqué.

• Work big!

• Allow for changes as the project continues.

This is where it started!

STEP 2: SELECT YOUR BACKGROUNDS

Part of the inspiration for this project was my desire to make a background using the plaid fabrics. I love a good plaid, and when I found these two pieces woven uniquely in Thailand, I just had to put them on the design wall.

The next obvious choice was Anna Maria Horner's Social Climber print for FreeSpirit Fabrics. The roses growing up the panel makes my heart sing. The Star Flower border just seemed to fit into the color scheme while adding another style of fabric.

Select fabrics that:

• Sit comfortably together but don't necessarily match.

• Have a style of their own (each one is a hero figure).

• Fit the space they are to take up.

Remember that random choices are sometimes the best.

I put the background together before starting the rest of the project.

Tip If your project is going to be very large, look for ways to do some appliqué on smaller sections first before you sew the entire quilt together!

STEP 3: DRAW FULL-SIZE PATTERN PIECES

Put your background up on the design wall and start making full-size pattern pieces for the major elements. Draw the shapes the size you desire using tracing paper. Pin them up on the background to be sure they are the shape and scale required. You may need to experiment with the sizes until you find what you like.

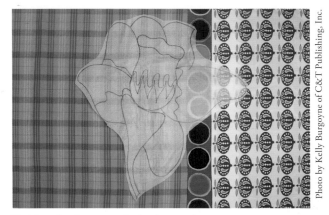

Position the shapes on the backgrounds.

Use a chalk pencil to draw in lines for vines or branches, or go ahead and make some bias vines (page 36) to play with. Remember to think about how you work the line. The stem is organic in nature and moves from wide to narrow as it reaches up. The diagonal line of the stem adds interest as well.

You may have to adapt as you go, but using the design wall gives you a chance to see how your sketch will play out on the background.

STEP 4: CHOOSING APPLIQUÉ FABRICS

I gathered some fabrics quickly so as not to overthink it. Here are some considerations:

• Will the fabric create the necessary line for the shape it is to become?

• Consider the values in your fabrics (arrange them in value scales as in Exercise 1: Analyzing Your Fabric Choices, page 25), and select fabrics that work from light to dark.

For example, in this quilt, the stem is the smallest shape on the busy background. To make it stand out, I gave it the darkest-value fabric. Use strong colors sparingly to create interest.

Value also is used to create the shadow areas in the flower and bud. Where fabrics tended to blend but needed a line, I added a small edge of darker fabric to the appliqué shape to create the line.

• The bigger shapes demand more careful consideration for how the pattern will play. Working with large-scale motifs presents different issues than smaller work. It takes some fabric auditioning to get the shapes to create the right impact without overpowering the shape itself. I looked for medium-density prints that didn't have strong motifs.

• Place the brightest elements in strategic locations. The yellow is the most dynamic, eye-catching part of my large flower. I intentionally placed it in the top third, or the *golden mean*, of the background.

When the tracing paper patterns are finalized, trace them onto wash-way appliqué paper and cut out to prepare the appliqué.

Take a photo of your fabric choices and convert it to black and white to see if the values work. Look for areas that might need dark accents to increase the contrast.

Some of the colors reference the real-life versions of the plant, and some just don't!

Tip Cut the lines of the drawing to reveal the individual shapes. It is then possible to further examine the fabric choices. Trace the shapes onto fabric with a chalk pencil and cut them out. Position them on the background and take a photo before doing the appliqué. This can be done with the seam allowance included. Or if you are very unsure and have enough fabric, cut the shapes to the finished size to see if it will work visually.

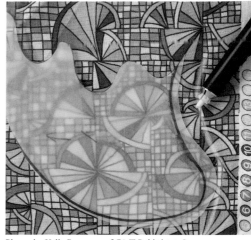

Photos by Kelly Burgoyne of C&T Publishing, Inc.

Making the Quilt

To make your own design experiment, use the following notes as a guide to purchasing materials, setting up the background, and selecting appliqué fabrics. The appliqué shapes are up to you!

MATERIALS

BACKGROUND FABRICS: Varying amounts based on the sizes of fabric pieces you choose. Mine were the following:

- **MAIN PIECE:** 25½″ × 47″
- **INNER VERTICAL STRIP:** 8½″ × 47″
- **OUTER VERTICAL STRIP:** 10½″ × 47″
- **BOTTOM STRIP:** 10½″ × 43½″

APPLIQUÉ FABRICS: Varying amounts based on your design

BACKING: Varies based on finished quilt size (I needed approximately 3 yards.)

BATTING: 4″ larger in each direction than your quilt top

BINDING: Varies based on finished quilt size (I needed just under ½ yard.)

TRACING PAPER

APPLIQUÉ SUPPLIES

1. Cut background fabrics if needed and sew together to make the background.

2. Prepare the appliqué pieces from the full-size pattern pieces you made and add them to the background.

3. Consider the variety of techniques for assembly offered and apply where necessary.

Quilting

This quilt is machine quilted with a clamshell-style pattern. You can draw the quilting line with chalk pencil and a 4″ circle template divided into quarters. Start by marking the first row of half-circles at the upper edge of the quilt. To draw the row below, align 1 set of quarter marks on the circle template with the bottom of the curves of 2 half-circles, and the other with the point between 2 half-circles. Continue across and down the quilt.

At the end of the day … it's quilting time!

acknowledgments

At the end of each book, I am reminded of how much my friends and coworkers bring the color of my life. We are all lucky to be quilters; it holds us together. I am nothing but a collection of the wonderful influences of the quilters in my life.

I am grateful for the design inspiration from my good friend Wendy Williams, who has a huge heart and endless talent. I also appreciate the other teachers in my shop. Susanne Cody has continuously reinvented herself, her use of fabric, and her techniques to bring creative ideas to life. Marg George leads quilters to new boundaries of self-expression with a timeless flair. Sue Ross brings an eclectic sense of mixing fabrics and tradition.

I am also grateful to the team at FreeSpirit Fabrics, including Anna Maria Horner, Kaffe Fassett, and Brandon Mably, for their constant inspiration, mentoring, and friendship—not to mention that Kaffe and Brandon put the binding on several of the quilts in this book!

And then there are the women of Material Obsession: Cath Babidge, my chief of everything and constant adviser on all things friend and business related; Helena Fooij, who is my honesty barometer; and Karen Johns, the voice of reason and intelligence. Anna Roberts is our life-support system—a combination of humor and organizational skills. Beverly Mason and Grace Widders bring their own flair and personality to managing the shop or classroom. Of course, eternal thanks to Carolyn Davis, who has been here since the beginning of Material Obsession adding a devil-may-care attitude to fabric combinations and design as well as a good neck rub.

I also gratefully acknowledge Karla Menaugh, my editor, who managed to make me feel like it was possible when I wasn't sure!

Then there is John … the "boss" at Material Obsession, doer of all things that need to be done and the only reason I can function at all. Thanks to him and my beautiful boys, Oscar, Noah, and Sam, for the stability of our family, our shared creative spirit, and the unconditional love.

about the author

Traveling to teach in my home country is a gift!

VISIT KATHY ONLINE AND
FOLLOW ON SOCIAL MEDIA!

WEBSITE: materialobsession.com.au
BLOG: materialobsession.typepad.com
FACEBOOK: Material Obsession
INSTAGRAM: @matobsgirl

Working together makes it happen!

Available as a Print-On-Demand
and eBook only

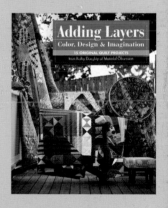

KATHY DOUGHTY is a self-taught quilter, author, fabric designer, and owner of Material Obsession since 2003. Material Obsession is a patchwork shop in Sydney, Australia, that is known for innovation in contemporary fabrics and designs. Working with customers, teachers, and industry leaders has given Kathy a unique skill base and an eclectic style.

As well as designing quilts and teaching, she also designs fabric for FreeSpirit Fabrics. Her collections bring to life drawings from her imagination in a format designed to be used in quilts. The color palettes bridge traditional and more contemporary trends.

She manages the growing business with her photographer husband, John, and a team of wonderfully creative women. Together they have produced five books, including *Material Obsession* and *Material Obsession 2*, as well as *Making Quilts with Kathy Doughty of Material Obsession*; *Adding Layers—Color, Design & Imagination*; and *Mixing Quilt Elements*. The books focus on getting the most interesting results from relatively easy techniques.

At home, Kathy has three grown sons in their twenties. They are all keenly interested in creative endeavors of their own, from making art to music. Kathy was born in the United States and worked in New York City for the duration of the 1980s in advertising, in fashion, and for the start-up Swatch Watch before moving to California for a year and then to Sydney, Australia, in 1990. She now calls Australia home but enjoys frequent trips to the United States to teach, go to Quilt Market, and visit family.

About the Author

EXPAND YOUR
art quilting

15 MINUTES OF PLAY
Improvisational Quilts

Victoria Findlay Wolfe

Made-Fabric Piecing • Traditional Blocks • Scrap Challenges

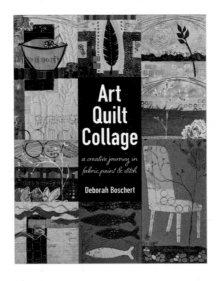

Art Quilt Collage

a creative journey in fabric, paint & stitch

Deborah Boschert

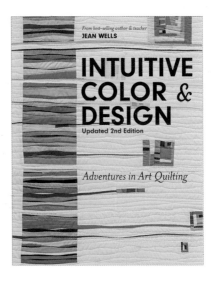

From best-selling author & teacher
JEAN WELLS

INTUITIVE COLOR & DESIGN
Updated 2nd Edition

Adventures in Art Quilting

Christina Cameli

Step-by-Step Tutorials
WEDGE QUILT WORKSHOP
10 Stunning Projects

MARIA SHELL
iMPROV PATCHWORK
Dynamic Quilts Made with Line & Shape

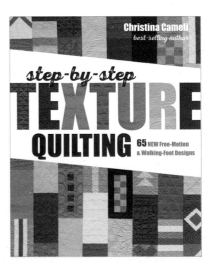

Christina Cameli
best-selling author

step-by-step TEXTURE QUILTING
65 NEW Free-Motion & Walking-Foot Designs